FREE Test Taking Tips DVD Offer

To help us better serve you, we have developed a Test Taking Tips DVD that we would like to give you for FREE. **This DVD covers world-class test taking tips that you can use to be even more successful when you are taking your test.**

All that we ask is that you email us your feedback about your study guide. Please let us know what you thought about it – whether that is good, bad or indifferent.

To get your **FREE Test Taking Tips DVD**, email freedvd@studyguideteam.com with "FREE DVD" in the subject line and the following information in the body of the email:

　　a. The title of your study guide.

　　b. Your product rating on a scale of 1-5, with 5 being the highest rating.

　　c. Your feedback about the study guide. What did you think of it?

　　d. Your full name and shipping address to send your free DVD.

If you have any questions or concerns, please don't hesitate to contact us at freedvd@studyguideteam.com.

Thanks again!

ISEE Lower Level Test Prep

ISEE Test Prep Lower Level Team

SSAT	ISEE
Verbal →	— Vocab, Math & Reading Comprehension
Difficult	
Math → Difficult	
Reading Comp. Fiction & Nonfiction	Nonfiction
Synonyms & Analogies	Synonyms & Sentence Completion — Vocab
Shorter, broader range of genres, incl. poetry	longer — Reading passages
	Mathematical reasoning — Math
SSAT	essay — not scored sent to school to which you apply
	2 hours — 30 min.

no penalty for wrong answers	Scores no penalty for wrong answers

Table of Contents

Quick Overview

As you draw closer to taking your exam, effective preparation becomes more and more important. Thankfully, you have this study guide to help you get ready. Use this guide to help keep your studying on track and refer to it often.

This study guide contains several key sections that will help you be successful on your exam. The guide contains tips for what you should do the night before and the day of the test. Also included are test-taking tips. Knowing the right information is not always enough. Many well-prepared test takers struggle with exams. These tips will help equip you to accurately read, assess, and answer test questions.

A large part of the guide is devoted to showing you what content to expect on the exam and to helping you better understand that content. Near the end of this guide is a practice test so that you can see how well you have grasped the content. Then, answer explanations are provided so that you can understand why you missed certain questions.

Don't try to cram the night before you take your exam. This is not a wise strategy for a few reasons. First, your retention of the information will be low. Your time would be better used by reviewing information you already know rather than trying to learn a lot of new information. Second, you will likely become stressed as you try to gain a large amount of knowledge in a short amount of time. Third, you will be depriving yourself of sleep. So be sure to go to bed at a reasonable time the night before. Being well-rested helps you focus and remain calm.

Be sure to eat a substantial breakfast the morning of the exam. If you are taking the exam in the afternoon, be sure to have a good lunch as well. Being hungry is distracting and can make it difficult to focus. You have hopefully spent lots of time preparing for the exam. Don't let an empty stomach get in the way of success!

When travelling to the testing center, leave earlier than needed. That way, you have a buffer in case you experience any delays. This will help you remain calm and will keep you from missing your appointment time at the testing center.

Be sure to pace yourself during the exam. Don't try to rush through the exam. There is no need to risk performing poorly on the exam just so you can leave the testing center early. Allow yourself to use all of the allotted time if needed.

Remain positive while taking the exam even if you feel like you are performing poorly. Thinking about the content you should have mastered will not help you perform better on the exam.

Once the exam is complete, take some time to relax. Even if you feel that you need to take the exam again, you will be well served by some down time before you begin studying again. It's often easier to convince yourself to study if you know that it will come with a reward!

Test-Taking Strategies

1. Predicting the Answer

When you feel confident in your preparation for a multiple-choice test, try predicting the answer before reading the answer choices. This is especially useful on questions that test objective factual knowledge or that ask you to fill in a blank. By predicting the answer before reading the available choices, you eliminate the possibility that you will be distracted or led astray by an incorrect answer choice. You will feel more confident in your selection if you read the question, predict the answer, and then find your prediction among the answer choices. After using this strategy, be sure to still read all of the answer choices carefully and completely. If you feel unprepared, you should not attempt to predict the answers. This would be a waste of time and an opportunity for your mind to wander in the wrong direction.

2. Reading the Whole Question

Too often, test takers scan a multiple-choice question, recognize a few familiar words, and immediately jump to the answer choices. Test authors are aware of this common impatience, and they will sometimes prey upon it. For instance, a test author might subtly turn the question into a negative, or he or she might redirect the focus of the question right at the end. The only way to avoid falling into these traps is to read the entirety of the question carefully before reading the answer choices.

3. Looking for Wrong Answers

Long and complicated multiple-choice questions can be intimidating. One way to simplify a difficult multiple-choice question is to eliminate all of the answer choices that are clearly wrong. In most sets of answers, there will be at least one selection that can be dismissed right away. If the test is administered on paper, the test taker could draw a line through it to indicate that it may be ignored; otherwise, the test taker will have to perform this operation mentally or on scratch paper. In either case, once the obviously incorrect answers have been eliminated, the remaining choices may be considered. Sometimes identifying the clearly wrong answers will give the test taker some information about the correct answer. For instance, if one of the remaining answer choices is a direct opposite of one of the eliminated answer choices, it may well be the correct answer. The opposite of obviously wrong is obviously right! Of course, this is not always the case. Some answers are obviously incorrect simply because they are irrelevant to the question being asked. Still, identifying and eliminating some incorrect answer choices is a good way to simplify a multiple-choice question.

4. Don't Overanalyze

Anxious test takers often overanalyze questions. When you are nervous, your brain will often run wild, causing you to make associations and discover clues that don't actually exist. If you feel that this may be a problem for you, do whatever you can to slow down during the test. Try taking a deep breath or counting to ten. As you read and consider the question, restrict yourself to the particular words used by the author. Avoid thought tangents about what the author *really* meant, or what he or she was *trying* to say. The only things that matter on a multiple-choice test are the words that are actually in the question. You must avoid reading too much into a multiple-choice question, or supposing that the writer meant something other than what he or she wrote.

5. No Need for Panic

It is wise to learn as many strategies as possible before taking a multiple-choice test, but it is likely that you will come across a few questions for which you simply don't know the answer. In this situation, avoid panicking. Because most multiple-choice tests include dozens of questions, the relative value of a single wrong answer is small. Moreover, your failure on one question has no effect on your success elsewhere on the test. As much as possible, you should compartmentalize each question on a multiple-choice test. In other words, you should not allow your feelings about one question to affect your success on the others. When you find a question that you either don't understand or don't know how to answer, just take a deep breath and do your best. Read the entire question slowly and carefully. Try rephrasing the question a couple of different ways. Then, read all of the answer choices carefully. After eliminating obviously wrong answers, make a selection and move on to the next question.

6. Confusing Answer Choices

When working on a difficult multiple-choice question, there may be a tendency to focus on the answer choices that are the easiest to understand. Many people, whether consciously or not, gravitate to the answer choices that require the least concentration, knowledge, and memory. This is a mistake. When you come across an answer choice that is confusing, you should give it extra attention. A question might be confusing because you do not know the subject matter to which it refers. If this is the case, don't eliminate the answer before you have affirmatively settled on another. When you come across an answer choice of this type, set it aside as you look at the remaining choices. If you can confidently assert that one of the other choices is correct, you can leave the confusing answer aside. Otherwise, you will need to take a moment to try to better understand the confusing answer choice. Rephrasing is one way to tease out the sense of a confusing answer choice.

7. Your First Instinct

Many people struggle with multiple-choice tests because they overthink the questions. If you have studied sufficiently for the test, you should be prepared to trust your first instinct once you have carefully and completely read the question and all of the answer choices. There is a great deal of research suggesting that the mind can come to the correct conclusion very quickly once it has obtained all of the relevant information. At times, it may seem to you as if your intuition is working faster even than your reasoning mind. This may in fact be true. The knowledge you obtain while studying may be retrieved from your subconscious before you have a chance to work out the associations that support it. Verify your instinct by working out the reasons that it should be trusted.

8. Key Words

Many test takers struggle with multiple-choice questions because they have poor reading comprehension skills. Quickly reading and understanding a multiple-choice question requires a mixture of skill and experience. To help with this, try jotting down a few key words and phrases on a piece of scrap paper. Doing this concentrates the process of reading and forces the mind to weigh the relative importance of the question's parts. In selecting words and phrases to write down, the test taker thinks about the question more deeply and carefully. This is especially true for multiple-choice questions that are preceded by a long prompt.

9. Subtle Negatives

One of the oldest tricks in the multiple-choice test writer's book is to subtly reverse the meaning of a question with a word like *not* or *except*. If you are not paying attention to each word in the question, you can easily be led astray by this trick. For instance, a common question format is, "Which of the following is…?" Obviously, if the question instead is, "Which of the following is not…?," then the answer will be quite different. Even worse, the test makers are aware of the potential for this mistake and will include one answer choice that would be correct if the question were not negated or reversed. A test taker who misses the reversal will find what he or she believes to be a correct answer and will be so confident that he or she will fail to reread the question and discover the original error. The only way to avoid this is to practice a wide variety of multiple-choice questions and to pay close attention to each and every word.

10. Reading Every Answer Choice

It may seem obvious, but you should always read every one of the answer choices! Too many test takers fall into the habit of scanning the question and assuming that they understand the question because they recognize a few key words. From there, they pick the first answer choice that answers the question they believe they have read. Test takers who read all of the answer choices might discover that one of the latter answer choices is actually *more* correct. Moreover, reading all of the answer choices can remind you of facts related to the question that can help you arrive at the correct answer. Sometimes, a misstatement or incorrect detail in one of the latter answer choices will trigger your memory of the subject and will enable you to find the right answer. Failing to read all of the answer choices is like not reading all of the items on a restaurant menu: you might miss out on the perfect choice.

11. Spot the Hedges

One of the keys to success on multiple-choice tests is paying close attention to every word. This is never more true than with words like *almost, most, some,* and *sometimes.* These words are called "hedges" because they indicate that a statement is not totally true or not true in every place and time. An absolute statement will contain no hedges, but in many subjects, like literature and history, the answers are not always straightforward or absolute. There are always exceptions to the rules in these subjects. For this reason, you should favor those multiple-choice questions that contain hedging language. The presence of qualifying words indicates that the author is taking special care with his or her words, which is certainly important when composing the right answer. After all, there are many ways to be wrong, but there is only one way to be right! For this reason, it is wise to avoid answers that are absolute when taking a multiple-choice test. An absolute answer is one that says things are either all one way or all another. They often include words like *every, always, best,* and *never.* If you are taking a multiple-choice test in a subject that doesn't lend itself to absolute answers, be on your guard if you see any of these words.

12. Long Answers

In many subject areas, the answers are not simple. As already mentioned, the right answer often requires hedges. Another common feature of the answers to a complex or subjective question are qualifying clauses, which are groups of words that subtly modify the meaning of the sentence. If the question or answer choice describes a rule to which there are exceptions or the subject matter is complicated, ambiguous, or confusing, the correct answer will require many words in order to be expressed clearly and accurately. In essence, you should not be deterred by answer choices that seem excessively long. Oftentimes, the author of the text will not be able to write the correct answer without offering some qualifications and modifications. Your job is to read the answer choices thoroughly and completely and to select the one that most accurately and precisely answers the question.

13. Restating to Understand

Sometimes, a question on a multiple-choice test is difficult not because of what it asks but because of how it is written. If this is the case, restate the question or answer choice in different words. This process serves a couple of important purposes. First, it forces you to concentrate on the core of the question. In order to rephrase the question accurately, you have to understand it well. Rephrasing the question will concentrate your mind on the key words and ideas. Second, it will present the information to your mind in a fresh way. This process may trigger your memory and render some useful scrap of information picked up while studying.

14. True Statements

Sometimes an answer choice will be true in itself, but it does not answer the question. This is one of the main reasons why it is essential to read the question carefully and completely before proceeding to the answer choices. Too often, test takers skip ahead to the answer choices and look for true statements. Having found one of these, they are content to select it without reference to the question above. Obviously, this provides an easy way for test makers to play tricks. The savvy test taker will always read the entire question before turning to the answer choices. Then, having settled on a correct answer choice, he or she will refer to the original question and ensure that the selected answer is relevant. The mistake of choosing a correct-but-irrelevant answer choice is especially common on questions related to specific pieces of objective knowledge, like historical or scientific facts. A prepared test taker will have a wealth of factual knowledge at his or her disposal, and should not be careless in its application.

15. No Patterns

One of the more dangerous ideas that circulates about multiple-choice tests is that the correct answers tend to fall into patterns. These erroneous ideas range from a belief that B and C are the most common right answers, to the idea that an unprepared test-taker should answer "A-B-A-C-A-D-A-B-A." It cannot be emphasized enough that pattern-seeking of this type is exactly the WRONG way to approach a multiple-choice test. To begin with, it is highly unlikely that the test maker will plot the correct answers according to some predetermined pattern. The questions are scrambled and delivered in a random order. Furthermore, even if the test maker was following a pattern in the assignation of correct answers, there is no reason why the test taker would know which pattern he or she was using. Any attempt to discern a pattern in the answer choices is a waste of time and a distraction from the real work of taking the test. A test taker would be much better served by extra preparation before the test than by reliance on a pattern in the answers.

FREE DVD OFFER

Don't forget that doing well on your exam includes both understanding the test content and understanding how to use what you know to do well on the test. We offer a completely FREE Test Taking Tips DVD that covers world class test taking tips that you can use to be even more successful when you are taking your test.

All that we ask is that you email us your feedback about your study guide. To get your **FREE Test Taking Tips DVD**, email freedvd@studyguideteam.com with "FREE DVD" in the subject line and the following information in the body of the email:

- The title of your study guide.
- Your product rating on a scale of 1-5, with 5 being the highest rating.
- Your feedback about the study guide. What did you think of it?
- Your full name and shipping address to send your free DVD.

Introduction to the ISEE Lower Exam

Function of the Test

The Lower Level ISEE (Independent School Entrance Exam) is a test, offered by the Educational Records Bureau (ERB), that is designed to be used for admission assessment at independent schools for entrance to fifth and sixth grades. Three other ISEE exams cover students seeking to enter other grades. Accordingly, the typical test taker is usually a prospective fifth or sixth grade student at a private school in the United States. The test is also used by a few international schools, primarily those catering to American parents.

ISEE scores are available to the test taker and to schools the test taker is seeking admission to. They are typically used only by such schools, and only as part of the admissions process.

Test Administration

The test is available in both computer and paper versions. The computer version can be taken online, allowing it to be administered at any time and date. The test may also be administered at ERB member schools, ERB offices, and any of 400 plus Prometric testing sites.

Upon arrival at the testing site, test takers present a verification letter or identification and get checked in. Test takers are encouraged to ask questions for clarification before the exam begins, as administrators are not permitted to discuss the test questions once testing begins. Test takers are asked to bring four #2 pencils and two pens.

Test takers may register for the Lower Level ISEE no more than three times during a given year, once each in any or all of three testing seasons. The testing seasons are fall (August through November), winter (December through March), and spring/summer (April through July). Reasonable accommodations are available for test takers with documented disabilities under the Americans with Disabilities Act.

Test Format

The content of the Lower Level ISEE is based on standards prepared by organizations including the National Council of Teachers of English, the International Reading Association, and the National Council of Teachers of Mathematics. The test consists of four multiple-choice sections and one essay section. A test taker's ISEE score is based on their performance on the four multiple choice sections. The essay is not graded, but is included with the scores when they are sent to a school. A breakdown of the sections is as follows:

Section	Content	Questions	Time
Verbal Reasoning	Multiple choice, scored	34	20
Quantitative Reasoning	Multiple choice, scored	38	35
Reading Comprehension	Multiple choice, scored	25	25
Mathematics Achievement	Multiple choice, scored	30	30
Essay	Written, unscored	NA	30

Scoring

Scores are based only on the number of correct answers provided. There is no penalty for guessing incorrectly, aside from the missed opportunity to provide another correct answer. That total number of correct answers becomes a raw score, which is then converted to a scaled score between 760 and 940. There is no set passing score on the exam. Instead, scores are reviewed by schools in conjunction with other factors in determining admissions decisions.

Scores are first provided to the test taker's family. The family may then decide whether to release the report to schools, and to which schools to release it. Scores may be received as soon as a couple days after completion of an exam.

Recent/Future Developments

ERB recently set the limit on retakes at one per testing season. It also instituted a rule allowing test takers' families to review scores before a school does.

Verbal Reasoning

Synonyms

Synonyms are words that mean the same or nearly the same if given a list of words in the same language. When presented with several words and asked to choose the synonym, more than one word may be similar to the original. However, one word is generally the strongest match. Synonyms should always share the same part of speech. For instance, *shy* and *timid* are both adjectives and hold similar meanings. The words *shy* and *loner* are similar, but shy is an adjective, while loner is a noun. Another way to test for the best synonym is to reread the quesetion with each possible word and determine which one makes the most sense. Consider the words: adore, sweet, kind, and nice.

Now consider the following sentence: *He will love you forever.*

He will adore you forever.

He will sweet you forever.

He will kind you forever.

He will nice you forever.

In the first sentence, the word *love* is used as a verb. The best synonym from the list that shares the same part of speech is *adore*. Adore is a verb, and when substituted in the sentence, it is the only substitution that makes grammatical and semantic sense.

Synonyms can be found for nouns, adjectives, verbs, adverbs, and prepositions. Here are some examples of synonyms from different parts of speech:

- Nouns: clothes, wardrobe, attire, apparel
- Verbs: run, spring, dash
- Adjectives: fast, quick, rapid, swift
- Adverbs: slowly, nonchalantly, leisurely
- Prepositions: near, proximal, neighboring, close

Here are several more examples of synonyms in the English language:

Word	Synonym	Meaning
smart	intelligent	having or showing a high level of intelligence
exact	specific	clearly identified
almost	nearly	not quite but very close
to annoy	to bother	to irritate
to answer	to reply	to form a written or verbal response
building	edifice	a structure that stands on its own with a roof and four walls
business	commerce	the act of purchasing, negotiating, trading, and selling
defective	faulty	when a device is not working or not working well

Vocabulary

In order to understand synonyms, one must have a good foundation of vocabulary. *Vocabulary* is the words a person uses on a daily basis. Having a good vocabulary is important. It's important in writing and also when you talk to people. Many of the questions on the test may have words that you don't know. Therefore, it's important to learn ways to find out a word's meaning.

It's hard to use vocabulary correctly. Imagine being thrust into a foreign country. If you didn't know right words to use to ask for the things you need, you could run into trouble! Asking for help from people who don't share the same vocabulary is hard. Language helps us understand each other. The more vocabulary words a person knows, the easier they can ask for things they need. This section of the study guide focuses on getting to know vocabulary through basic grammar.

Prefixes and Suffixes

In this section, we will look at the *meaning* of various prefixes and suffixes when added to a root word. A *prefix* is a combination of letters found at the beginning of a word. A *suffix* is a combination of letters found at the end. A *root word* is the word that comes after the prefix, before the suffix, or between them both. Sometimes a root word can stand on its own without either a prefix or a suffix. More simply put:

Prefix + Root Word = Word

Root Word + Suffix = Word

Prefix + Root Word + Suffix = Word

Root Word = Word

Knowing the definitions of common prefixes and suffixes is helpful. It's helpful when you are trying to find out the meaning of a word you don't know. Also, knowing prefixes can help you find out the number of things, the negative of something, or the time and space of an object! Understanding suffixes can help when trying to find out the meaning of an adjective, noun, or verb.

The following charts look at some of the most common prefixes, what they mean, and how they're used to find out a word's meaning:

Number and Quantity Prefixes

Prefix	Definition	Example
bi-	two	bicycle, bilateral
mono-	one, single	monopoly, monotone
poly-	many	polygamy, polygon
semi-	half, partly	semiannual, semicircle
uni-	one	unicycle, universal

Here's an example of a number prefix:

The girl rode on a *bicycle* to school.

Look at the word *bicycle*. The root word (*cycle*)comes from the Greek and means *wheel*. The prefix *bi-* means *two*. The word *bicycle* means two wheels! When you look at any bicycles, they all have two wheels. If you had a unicycle, your bike would only have one wheel, because *uni-* means *one*.

Negative Prefixes

Prefix	Definition	Example
a-	without, lack of	amoral, atypical
in-	not, opposing	inability, inverted
non-	not	nonexistent, nonstop
un-	not, reverse	unable, unspoken

Here's an example of a negative prefix:

The girl was *insensitive* to the boy who broke his leg.

Look at the word *insensitive*. In the chart above, the prefix *in-* means *not* or *opposing*. Replace the prefix with *not*. Now place *not* in front of the word *sensitive*. Now we see that the girl was "not sensitive" to the boy who broke his leg. In simpler terms, she showed that she did not care. These are easy ways to use prefixes and suffixes in order to find out what a word means.

Time and Space Prefixes

Prefix	Definition	Example
a-	in, on, of, up, to	aloof, associate
ab-	from, away, off	abstract, absent
ad-	to, towards	adept, adjacent
ante-	before, previous	antebellum, antenna
anti-	against, opposing	anticipate, antisocial
cata-	down, away, thoroughly	catacomb, catalogue
circum-	around	circumstance, circumvent
com-	with, together, very	combine, compel
contra-	against, opposing	contraband, contrast
de-	from	decrease, descend
dia-	through, across, apart	diagram, dialect
dis-	away, off, down, not	disregard, disrespect
epi-	upon	epidemic, epiphany
ex-	out	example, exit
hypo-	under, beneath	hypoallergenic, hypothermia
inter-	among, between	intermediate, international
intra-	within	intrapersonal, intravenous
ob-	against, opposing	obtain, obscure
per-	through	permanent, persist
peri-	around	periodontal, periphery
post-	after, following	postdate, postoperative
pre-	before, previous	precede, premeditate
pro-	forward, in place of	program, propel
retro-	back, backward	retroactive, retrofit
sub-	under, beneath	submarine, substantial
super-	above, extra	superior, supersede
trans-	across, beyond, over	transform, transmit
ultra-	beyond, excessively	ultraclean, ultralight

Here's an example of a space prefix:

> The teacher's motivational speech helped *propel* her students toward greater academic achievement.

Look at the word *propel*. The prefix *pro-* means *forward*. *Forward* means something related to time and space. *Propel* means to drive or move in a forward direction. Therefore, knowing the prefix *pro-* helps interpret that the students are moving forward *toward greater academic achievement*.

Miscellaneous Prefixes

Prefix	Definition	Example
belli-	war, warlike	bellied, belligerent
bene-	well, good	benediction, beneficial
equi-	equal	equidistant, equinox
for-	away, off, from	forbidden, forsaken
fore-	previous	forecast, forebode
homo-	same, equal	homogeneous, homonym
hyper-	excessive, over	hyperextend, hyperactive
in-	in, into	insignificant, invasive
magn-	large	magnetic, magnificent
mal-	bad, poorly, not	maladapted, malnourished
mis-	bad, poorly, not	misplace, misguide
mor-	death	mortal, morgue
neo-	new	neoclassical, neonatal
omni-	all, everywhere	omnipotent, omnipresent
ortho-	right, straight	orthodontist, orthopedic
over-	above	overload, overstock,
pan-	all, entire	panacea, pander
para-	beside, beyond	paradigm, parameter
phil-	love, like	philanthropy, philosophic
prim-	first, early	primal, primer
re-	backward, again	reload, regress
sym-	with, together	symmetry, symbolize
vis-	to see	visual, visibility

Here's another prefix example:

> The computer was *primitive*; it still had a floppy disk drive!

The word *primitive* has the prefix *prim-*. The prefix *prim-*indicates being *first* or *early*. *Primitive* means the early stages of evolution. It also could mean the historical development of something. Therefore, the sentence is saying that the computer is an older model, because it still has a floppy disk drive.

The charts that follow review some of the most common suffixes. They also include examples of how the suffixes are used to determine the meaning of a word. Remember, suffixes are added to the *end* of a root word:

Adjective Suffixes

Suffix	Definition	Example
-able (-ible)	capable of being	teachable, accessible
-esque	in the style of, like	humoresque, statuesque
-ful	filled with, marked by	helpful, deceitful
-ic	having, containing	manic, elastic
-ish	suggesting, like	malnourish, tarnish
-less	lacking, without	worthless, fearless
-ous	marked by, given to	generous, previous

Here's an example of an adjective suffix:

The live model looked so *statuesque* in the window display; she didn't even move!

Look at the word *statuesque*. The suffix *-esque* means *in the style of* or *like*. If something is *statuesque*, it's *like a statue*. In this sentence, the model looks like a statue.

Noun Suffixes

Suffix	Definition	Example
-acy	state, condition	literacy, legacy
-ance	act, condition, fact	distance, importance
-ard	one that does	leotard, billiard
-ation	action, state, result	legislation, condemnation
-dom	state, rank, condition	freedom, kingdom
-er (-or)	office, action	commuter, spectator
-ess	feminine	caress, princess
-hood	state, condition	childhood, livelihood
-ion	action, result, state	communion, position
-ism	act, manner, doctrine	capitalism, patriotism
-ist	worker, follower	stylist, activist
-ity (-ty)	state, quality, condition	community, dirty
-ment	result, action	empowerment, segment
-ness	quality, state	fitness, rudeness
-ship	position	censorship, leadership
-sion (-tion)	state, result	tension, transition
-th	act, state, quality	twentieth, wealth
-tude	quality, state, result	attitude, latitude

Look at the following example of a noun suffix:

The *spectator* cheered when his favorite soccer team scored a goal.

Look at the word *spectator*. The suffix *-or* means *action*. In this sentence, the *action* is to *spectate* (watch something). Therefore, a *spectator* is someone involved in watching something.

Verb Suffixes

Suffix	Definition	Example
-ate	having, showing	facilitate, integrate
-en	cause to be, become	frozen, written
-fy	make, cause to have	modify, rectify
-ize	cause to be, treat with	realize, sanitize

Here's an example of a verb suffix:

The preschool had to *sanitize* the toys every Tuesday and Thursday.

In the word *sanitize*, the suffix *-ize* means *cause to be* or *treat with*. By adding the suffix *-ize* to the root word *sanitary*, the meaning of the word becomes active: *cause to be sanitary*.

Sentence Completion

Context Clues

It's common to find words that aren't familiar in writing. When you don't know a word, there are some "tricks" that can be used to find out its meaning. *Context clues* are words or phrases in a sentence or paragraph that provide hints about a word and what it means. For example, if an unknown word is attached to a noun with other surrounding words as clues, these can help you figure out the word's meaning. Consider the following example:

After the treatment, Grandma's natural rosy cheeks looked *wan* and ghostlike.

The word we don't know is *wan*. The first clue to its meaning is in the phrase *After the treatment,* which tells us that something happened after a procedure (possibly medical). A second clue is the word *rosy*, which describes Grandma's natural cheek color that changed after the treatment. Finally, the word *ghostlike* infers that Grandma's cheeks now look white. By using the context clues in the sentence, we can figure out that the meaning of the word *wan* means *pale*.

Below are more ways to use context clues to find out the meaning of a word we don't know:

Contrasts
Look for context clues that *contrast* the unknown word. When reading a sentence with a word we don't know, look for an opposite word or idea. Here's an example:

Since Mary didn't cite her research sources, she lost significant points for *plagiarizing* the content of her report.

In this sentence, *plagiarizing* is the word we don't know. Notice that when Mary *didn't cite her research sources,* it resulted in her losing points for *plagiarizing the content of her report*. These contrasting ideas tell us that Mary did something wrong with the content. This makes sense because the definition of *plagiarizing* is "taking the work of someone else and passing it off as your own."

Contrasts often use words like *but, however, although,* or phrases like *on the other hand.* For example:

The *gargantuan* television won't fit in my car, but it will cover the entire wall in the den.

The word we don't know is *gargantuan*. Notice that the television is too big to fit in a car, *but it will cover the entire wall in the den*. This tells us that the television is extremely large. The word *gargantuan* means *enormous*.

Synonyms
Another way to find out a word you don't know is to think of synonyms for that word. Synonyms are words with the same meaning. To do this, replace synonyms one at a time. Then read the sentence after each synonym to see if the meaning is clear. By replacing a word we don't know with a word we do know, it's easier to uncover its meaning. For example:

Gary's clothes were *saturated* after he fell into the swimming pool.

In this sentence, we don't know the word *saturated*. To brainstorm synonyms for *saturated*, think about what happens to Gary's clothes after falling into the swimming pool. They'd be *soaked* or *wet*. These both turn out to be good synonyms to try. The actual meaning of *saturated* is "thoroughly soaked."

Antonyms
Sometimes sentences contain words or phrases that oppose each other. Opposite words are known as *antonyms*. An example of an antonym is *hot* and *cold*. For example:

Although Mark seemed *tranquil*, you could tell he was actually nervous as he paced up and down the hall.

The word we don't know is *tranquil*. The sentence says that Mark was in fact not *tranquil*. He was *actually nervous*. The opposite of the word *nervous* is *calm*. *Calm* is the meaning of the word *tranquil*.

Explanations or Descriptions
Explanations or descriptions of other things in the sentence can also provide clues to an unfamiliar word. Take the following example:

Golden Retrievers, Great Danes, and Pugs are the top three *breeds* competing in the dog show.

We don't know the word *breeds*. Look at the sentence for a clue. The subjects (*Golden Retrievers, Great Danes,* and *Pugs*) describe different types of dogs. This description helps uncover the meaning of the word *breeds*. The word *breeds* means "a particular type of animal."

Inferences
Inferences are clues to an unknown word that tell us its meaning. These inferences can be found within the sentence where the word appears. Or, they can be found in a sentence before the word or after the word. Look at the following example:

The *wretched* old lady was kicked out of the restaurant. She was so mean and nasty to the waiter!

Here, we don't know the word *wretched*. The first sentence says that the *old lady was kicked out of the restaurant*, but it doesn't say why. The sentence after tells us why: *She was so mean and nasty to the waiter!* This infers that the old lady was *kicked out* because she was *so mean and nasty* or, in other words, *wretched*.

When you prepare for a vocabulary test, try reading harder materials to learn new words. If you don't know a word on the test, look for prefixes and suffixes to find out what the word means and get rid of wrong answers. If two answers both seem right, see if there are any differences between them. Then select the word that best fits. Context clues in the sentence or paragraph can also help you find the meaning of a word you don't know. By learning new words, a person can expand their knowledge. They can also improve the quality of their writing.

Practice Questions

Synonyms

Each of the questions below has one word. The one word is followed by five words or phrases. Please select one answer whose meaning is closest to the word in capital letters.

1. WEARY:
   a. tired
   b. clothing
   c. happy
   d. whiny

2. VAST:
   a. Rapid
   b. Expansive
   c. Small
   d. Ocean

3. DEMONSTRATE:
   a. Tell
   b. Show
   c. Build
   d. Complete

4. ORCHARD:
   a. Farm
   b. Fruit
   c. Grove
   d. Peach

5. TEXTILE:
   a. Fabric
   b. Knit
   c. Mural
   d. Ornament

6. OFFSPRING:
   a. Bounce
   b. Parent
   c. Music
   d. Child

7. PERMIT:
   a. Law
   b. Parking
   c. Crab
   d. Allow

8. INSPIRE:
   a. Motivate
   b. Impale
   c. Exercise
   d. Patronize

9. WOMAN:
   a. Man
   b. Lady
   c. Women
   d. Mother

10. ROTATION:
   a. Wheel
   b. Year
   c. Spin
   d. Flip

11. CONSISTENT:
   a. Steady
   b. Contains
   c. Sticky
   d. Texture

12. PRINCIPLE:
   a. Principal
   b. Leader
   c. President
   d. Foundation

13. PERIMETER:
   a. Outline
   b. Area
   c. Side
   d. Volume

14. SYMBOL:
   a. Drum
   b. Music   cymbal x
   c. Clang
   d. Emblem

15. GERMINATE:
   a. Doctor
   b. Sick
   c. Grow
   d. Plants

16. OPPRESSED:
    a. Acclaimed
    b. Helpless
    c. Beloved
    d. Pressured

17. TRIUMPH:
    a. Celebration
    b. Burial
    c. Animosity
    d. Banter

Sentence Completion

Select the word or phrase that most correctly completes the sentence.

18. When the baseball game was over, the first thing Jackson did was run towards the dugout to grab his water bottle to relieve his _____ throat.
    a. humid
    b. scorched
    c. parched
    d. dusty

19. Driving across the United States, the two friends became _____ each time they arrived in a new state. They shared many good memories on that trip they would remember for the rest of their lives.
    a. closer
    b. distant
    c. suffering
    d. irritable

20. After Kira wrote her first book, she _____ her fans the sequel would be just as exciting as the first.
    a. denied
    b. promised
    c. invigorated
    d. germinated

21. When I heard the wolf howl from my tent, my hands started _____ and my heart stopped . . . hopefully I would make it through this night alive!
    a. dancing
    b. glowing
    c. shaking
    d. throbbing

22. Unlike Leo, who always played basketball in the park after school, Gabriel _____.
    a. ate his lunch in the cafeteria.
    b. rode his bike to school in the morning.
    c. would swim in the park after school.
    d. would usually go to the library and study after school.

20

23. As soon as the shot rang out, the runners _____ toward the finish line.
   a. sprinted
   b. skipped
   c. rejoiced
   d. herded

24. Determined to get an *A* on her paper, LaShonda _____.
   a. went to the gym everyday for a month.
   b. taught her little brother how to read.
   c. learned how to speak Spanish and French.
   d. began writing it two weeks before it was due.

25. After Colby's mom picked him up from school, they went to the bank to _____ a check.
   a. celebrate
   b. neutralize
   c. eliminate
   d. deposit

26. The sale at the grocery store _____ my dad to buy four avocados instead of two.
   a. intimidated
   b. inspired
   c. dismayed
   d. berated

27. My mom recently started drinking fruit and vegetable smoothies in order to _____.
   a. increase the quality of her health.
   b. obtain a raise at her new insurance job.
   c. prove to herself that she could hike the Appalachian trail.
   d. encourage her sister to start working out at the gym with her.

28. When Lindsay asked me to _____ her party, I immediately began writing a list of the birthday presents she might like to receive.
   a. acclaim
   b. astound
   c. attend
   d. amend

29. Cooking dinner was her favorite activity until she _____ the fire alarm by burning the casserole in the oven.
   a. activated
   b. offended
   c. unplugged
   d. disbanded

30. Before she arrived at the _____ dentist's office to take care of a cavity, she did some breathing exercises and made sure her teeth were clean.
   a. refreshing
   b. creative
   c. rapturous
   d. dreaded

31. The yellow feathers and purple markings told us that this bird was _____ to the southeast part of the United States.
    a. entertaining
    b. indigenous
    c. impudent
    d. monotonous

32. Ever since the bus changed its route from Anna's house to the other side of town, _____.
    a. Anna started receiving better grades.
    b. Anna became afraid of the rain.
    c. Anna began riding her bike to school.
    d. Anna proved to her friend she could beat her in Ping-Pong.

33. When we caught the eels, their bodies _____ out of our hands and back into the water.
    a. exploded
    b. deteriorated
    c. thundered
    d. slithered

34. Even though at the restaurant my mom _____ the eggplant with no cheese, she received a huge serving of parmesan on top.
    a. requested
    b. directed
    c. mourned
    d. endorsed

Answer Explanations

1. A: Weary most closely means tired. Someone who is weary and tired may be whiny, but they do not necessarily mean the same thing.

2. B: Something that is vast is big and expansive. Choice *D*, ocean, may be described as vast. However, the word itself does not mean vast. The heavens or skies may also be described as vast. Someone's imagination or vocabulary can also be vast.

3. B: To demonstrate something means to show it. A demonstration is a show-and-tell type of example. It is usually visual.

4. C: An orchard is most like a grove. Both are areas like plantations that grow different kinds of fruit. Peach is a type of fruit that may be grown in an orchard. However, *peach* is not a synonym for orchard. Many citrus fruits are grown in groves. But either word can be used to describe many fruit-bearing trees in one area. Choice *A*, farm, may have an orchard or grove on the property. However, they are not the same thing, and many farms do not grow fruit trees.

5. A: A textile is another word for a fabric. The most confusing choice in this case is Choice *B*, knit. This is because some textiles are knit, but *textile* and *knit* are not synonyms. Plenty of textiles are not knit.

6. D: Offspring are the kids of parents. This word is common when talking about the animal kingdom, though it can be used with humans as well. *Offspring* does have the word *spring* in it. But it has nothing to do with bounce, Choice *A*. Choice *B*, parent, maybe tricky because parents have offspring. But for this reason, they are not synonyms.

7. D: Permit can be a verb or a noun. As a verb, it means to allow or give permission for something. As a noun, it refers to a document or something that has been authorized like a parking permit or driving permit. This would allow the authorized person to park or drive under the rules of the document.

8. A: If someone is inspired, they are driven to do something. Someone who is an inspiration motivates others to follow their lead.

9. B: A woman is a lady. You must read carefully and remember the difference between *woman* and *women*. *Woman* refers to one person who is female. *Women* is the plural form and refers to more than one, or a group, of ladies. A woman can be a mother, but not necessarily. *Woman* and *mother* are not synonyms.

10. C: Rotation means to spin or turn, like a wheel rotating on a car. But *wheel*, Choice *A*, does not mean the same thing as the word *rotation*.

11. A: Something that is consistent is steady, predictable, reliable, or constant. The tricky ones here is that the word *consistency* comes from the word consistent. *Consistency* may describe a texture or something that is sticky, Choices *C* and *D*. *Consistent* also comes from the word *consist*. *Consist* means to contain (Choice *B*).

12. D: A principle is a guiding idea or belief. Someone with good moral character is described as having strong principles. You must be careful not to get confused with the homonyms *principle* and *principal*, Choice *A*. These two words have different meanings. A principal is the leader of a school. The word principal also refers to the main idea or most important thing.

13. A: Perimeter refers to the outline of an object. You may recognize that word from math class. In math class, perimeter refers to the edges or distance around a closed shape. Some of the other choices refer to other math words encountered in geometry. However, they do not have the same meaning as *perimeter.*

14. D: A symbol is an object, picture, or sign that is used to represent something. For example, a pink ribbon is a symbol for breast-cancer awareness. A flag can be a symbol for a country. The tricky part of this question was also knowing the meaning of *emblem. Emblem* describes a design that represents a group or concept, much like a symbol. Emblems often appear on flags or a coat of arms.

15. C: Germinate means to develop or grow. It most often refers to sprouting seeds as a new plant first breaks through the seed coat. It can also refer to the development of an idea. Choice *D, plants,* may be an attractive choice since plants germinate. However, the word *germinate* does not mean *plant.*

16. B: The word *oppressed* means being exploited or helpless, Choice *B.* Choice *A,* acclaimed, means being praised. To be beloved, choice *C,* means to be cherished and adored. To be pressured, Choice *D,* means to be pushed into doing something, in some contexts.

17. A: The word triumph most closely means celebration, Choice *A.* Burial, Choice *B,* is the act of burying the dead. Animosity, Choice *C,* means strong dislike or hatred, and is very different from the word *triumph.* Choice *D,* banter, is the act of teasing.

18. C: Jackson wanted to relieve his *parched* throat. *Parched* is the correct answer because it means *thirsty.* Choice *A,* humid, means moist, and usually refers to the weather. Choice *B,* scorched, means blackened or baked, and doesn't fit in this context. While Jackson's throat could have been dusty, Choice *D,* from playing baseball, one usually doesn't need to relieve a dusty throat, but instead clean it.

19. A: The two friends became closer. For this question, it's important to look at the context of the sentence. The second sentence says the friends shared good memories on the trip, which would not make the friends distant or irritable, Choices *B* and *D.* Choice *C* does not grammatically fit within the sentence: "became suffering" is incorrect usage. Therefore, Choice *A* is correct.

20. B: She promised her fans the sequel would be just as exciting as the first. Choice *A,* denied, is the opposite of the word *promised* and does not fit with the word *excited.* Choice *C,* invigorated, means energized, and might fit the tone of the sentence with the word *excited.* However, *promised* is the better word to use here. Choice *D,* germinated, means to grow.

21. C: My hands started shaking and my heart stopped. Usually when someone is afraid or nervous, their hands start to shake. Choice *A,* dancing, does not make sense in the context of the sentence. Choice *B,* glowing, is incorrect; hands usually do not glow when one is afraid of something. Choice *D,* throbbing, is closer than *A* or *B,* but Choice *C,* shaking, is a better answer than *throbbing.*

22. D: Gabriel would usually go to the library and study after school. The word *unlike* tells us that Gabriel would do the opposite of what Leo would do at the time. Choices *A* and *B* talk about different times, in the morning and at lunch, so they are not the best answer choice here. Choice *C* is more similar to what Leo would do than Choice *D,* so Choice *D* is the correct choice.

23. A: The runners sprinted toward the finish line. Choice *B* is incorrect; runners who begin a race usually don't skip toward the finish line. Choice *C* does not fit within the context of the sentence, as normally runners would be *sprinting* and not *rejoicing* toward a finish line. Choice *D*, herded, means to gather around something; usually *herded* is used for animals and not for runners.

24. D: LaShonda began writing it two weeks before it was due. Choices *A, B,* and *C* all reference activities that don't have anything to do with writing a paper. If her paper was about any one of these things, like going to the gym or teaching someone to read, then perhaps these would be decent answers. However, we are not given enough information to know what the topic of the paper is. Therefore, Choice *D* is the correct answer.

25. D: They went to the bank to deposit a check. When people go to the bank with a check, they usually don't celebrate it, Choice *A*, but do something more practical with it, like deposit it. Choice *B*, neutralize, means to counteract something, and is incorrect in this sentence. Choice *C*, eliminate, means to get rid of something, and is also incorrect here.

26. B: The sale at the grocery store inspired my dad to buy four avocados instead of two. The word *inspired* means to encourage or stimulate. Sales are usually seen as a positive experience, so the sale *inspired* the dad to buy more avocados. The rest of the words (intimidated, dismayed, and berated) have negative connotations and therefore do not fit within the context of the sentence.

27. A: In order to increase the quality of her health. This phrase makes the most sense within the context of the sentence. Becoming healthier is a direct effect of consuming fruits and vegetables, so Choice *A* is the best answer choice here. Becoming healthier might lead to Choices *B, C,* and *D*, but these are not the best answers for this question.

28. C: When Lindsay asked me to attend her party. Choice *A*, acclaim, is an expression of approval, and is not the right fit here. Choice *B*, astound, means to amaze. Usually we don't hear of people "amazing" other people's parties. This is not the best choice. Choice *D*, amend, means to improve or correct. Again, this is not the best choice for the context; the speaker is wondering what gift to bring Lindsay, and is not thinking about ways to correct the party.

29. A: Until she activated the fire alarm by burning the casserole in the oven. Choice *B*, offended, is the wrong choice here. You can offend a person because they have emotions, but you cannot offend a fire alarm. Choice *C*, unplugged, is also incorrect. You cannot unplug a fire alarm by burning a casserole. Choice *D*, disbanded, is the opposite of *activated* and is incorrect in this context.

30. D: Before she arrived at the dreaded dentist's office. Choice *A*, refreshing, is not an adjective used to describe a dentist's office, especially when the patient is about to take care of a cavity. Choices *B*, creative, also does not fit within the context of the sentence. Choice *C*, rapturous, means ecstatic or happy, and is the opposite sentiment of what we are looking for.

31. B: Told us that the bird was indigenous to the southeast part of the United States. Indigenous means native to a certain area, so Choice *B* is the best answer here. Choice *A*, entertaining, does not make sense within this context. Choice *C*, impudent, means bold or shameless. Choice *D*, monotonous, means remaining the same or dull. These latter two answer choices are not the best fit for this context.

32. C: Anna began riding her bike to school. This question determines whether or not you can understand the nature of cause and effect. Choices *A, B,* and *D* could possibly be in a chain of events of effects from the bus taking a different route. However, the most direct cause is Choice *C*.

33. D: Their bodies slithered out of our hands and back into the water. Choices *A* and *C*, exploded and thundered, are too extreme for the context. Deteriorated, Choice *B*, means to crumble or disintegrate, which is not something an eel's body is likely to do on its own. Choice *D* is the best answer for this sentence.

34. A: My mom requested the eggplant with no cheese. Directed, Choice *B*, means to supervise or conduct, and does not make sense in the context of the sentence. Choice *C*, mourned, means to grieve over, and is also incorrect. Choice *D*, endorsed, means to approve or support something. Pay attention to words like *even though* that suggest a contrast of surprising facts.

Quantitative Reasoning and Math Achievement

Numbers and Operations

Base-10 Numerals, Number Names, and Expanded Form

Numbers used in everyday life are constituted in a base-10 system. Each digit in a number, depending on its location, represents some multiple of 10, or quotient of 10 when dealing with decimals. Each digit to the left of the decimal point represents a higher multiple of 10. Each digit to the right of the decimal point represents a quotient of a higher multiple of 10 for the divisor. For example, consider the number 7,631.42. The digit one represents simply the number one. The digit 3 represents 3×10. The digit 6 represents $6 \times 10 \times 10$ (or 6×100). The digit 7 represents $7 \times 10 \times 10 \times 10$ (or 7×1000). The digit 4 represents $4 \div 10$. The digit 2 represents $(2 \div 10) \div 10$, or $2 \div (10 \times 10)$ or $2 \div 100$.

A number is written in expanded form by expressing it as the sum of the value of each of its digits. The expanded form in the example above, which is written with the highest value first down to the lowest value, is expressed as: $7,000 + 600 + 30 + 1 + .4 + .02$.

When verbally expressing a number, the integer part of the number (the numbers to the left of the decimal point) resembles the expanded form without the addition between values. In the above example, the numbers read "seven thousand six hundred thirty-one." When verbally expressing the decimal portion of a number, the number is read as a whole number, followed by the place value of the furthest digit (non-zero) to the right. In the above example, 0.42 is read "forty-two hundredths." Reading the number 7,631.42 in its entirety is expressed as "seven thousand six hundred thirty-one and forty-two hundredths." The word *and* is used between the integer and decimal parts of the number.

Composing and Decomposing Multi-Digit Numbers

Composing and decomposing numbers aids in conceptualizing what each digit of a multi-digit number represents. The standard, or typical, form in which numbers are written consists of a series of digits representing a given value based on their place value. Consider the number 592.7. This number is composed of 5 hundreds, 9 tens, 2 ones, and 7 tenths.

Composing a number requires adding the given numbers for each place value and writing the numbers in standard form. For example, composing 4 thousands, 5 hundreds, 2 tens, and 8 ones consists of adding as follows: $4,000 + 500 + 20 + 8$, to produce 4,528 (standard form).

Decomposing a number requires taking a number written in standard form and breaking it apart into the sum of each place value. For example, the number 83.17 is decomposed by breaking it into the sum of 4 values (for each of the 4 digits): 8 tens, 3 ones, 1 tenth, and 7 hundredths. The decomposed or "expanded" form of 83.17 is $80 + 3 + .1 + .07$.

Place Value of a Given Digit

The number system that is used consists of only ten different digits or characters. However, this system is used to represent an infinite number of values. The place value system makes this infinite number of values possible. The position in which a digit is written corresponds to a given value. Starting from the decimal point (which is implied, if not physically present), each subsequent place value to the left represents a value greater than the one before it. Conversely, starting from the decimal point, each subsequent place value to the right represents a value less than the one before it.

The names for the place values to the left of the decimal point are as follows:

...	Billions	Hundred-Millions	Ten-Millions	Millions	Hundred-Thousands	Ten-Thousands	Thousands	Hundreds	Tens	Ones

*Note that this table can be extended infinitely further to the left.

The names for the place values to the right of the decimal point are as follows:

Decimal Point (.)	Tenths	Hundredths	Thousandths	Ten-Thousandths	...

*Note that this table can be extended infinitely further to the right.

When given a multi-digit number, the value of each digit depends on its place value. Consider the number 682,174.953. Referring to the chart above, it can be determined that the digit 8 is in the ten-thousands place. It is in the fifth place to the left of the decimal point. Its value is 8 ten-thousands or 80,000. The digit 5 is two places to the right of the decimal point. Therefore, the digit 5 is in the hundredths place. Its value is 5 hundredths or $\frac{5}{100}$ (equivalent to .05).

Base-10 System

Value of Digits
In accordance with the base-10 system, the value of a digit increases by a factor of ten each place it moves to the left. For example, consider the number 7. Moving the digit one place to the left (70), increases its value by a factor of 10 ($7 \times 10 = 70$). Moving the digit two places to the left (700) increases its value by a factor of 10 twice ($7 \times 10 \times 10 = 700$). Moving the digit three places to the left (7,000) increases its value by a factor of 10 three times ($7 \times 10 \times 10 \times 10 = 7,000$), and so on.

Conversely, the value of a digit decreases by a factor of ten each place it moves to the right. (Note that multiplying by $\frac{1}{10}$ is equivalent to dividing by 10). For example, consider the number 40. Moving the digit one place to the right (4) decreases its value by a factor of 10 ($40 \div 10 = 4$). Moving the digit two places to the right (0.4), decreases its value by a factor of 10 twice ($40 \div 10 \div 10 = 0.4$) or ($40 \times \frac{1}{10} \times \frac{1}{10} = 0.4$). Moving the digit three places to the right (0.04) decreases its value by a factor of 10 three times ($40 \div 10 \div 10 \div 10 = 0.04$) or ($40 \times \frac{1}{10} \times \frac{1}{10} \times \frac{1}{10} = 0.04$), and so on.

Exponents to Denote Powers of 10
The value of a given digit of a number in the base-10 system can be expressed utilizing powers of 10. A power of 10 refers to 10 raised to a given exponent such as 10^0, 10^1, 10^2, 10^3, etc. For the number 10^3, 10 is the base and 3 is the exponent. A base raised by an exponent represents how many times the base is multiplied by itself. Therefore, $10^1 = 10$, $10^2 = 10 \times 10 = 100$, $10^3 = 10 \times 10 \times 10 = 1,000$, $10^4 = 10 \times 10 \times 10 \times 10 = 10,000$, etc. Any base with a zero exponent equals one.

Powers of 10 are utilized to decompose a multi-digit number without writing all the zeroes. Consider the number 872,349. This number is decomposed to $800,000 + 70,000 + 2,000 + 300 + 40 + 9$. When utilizing powers of 10, the number 872,349 is decomposed to $(8 \times 10^5) + (7 \times 10^4) + (2 \times 10^3) + (3 \times 10^2) + (4 \times 10^1) + (9 \times 10^0)$. The power of 10 by which the digit is multiplied corresponds to the number of zeroes following the digit when expressing its value in standard form. For example, 7×10^4 is equivalent to 70,000 or 7 followed by four zeros.

Rounding Multi-Digit Numbers #4 TODO

Rounding numbers changes the given number to a simpler and less accurate number than the exact given number. Rounding allows for easier calculations which estimate the results of using the exact given number. The accuracy of the estimate and ease of use depends on the place value to which the number is rounded. Rounding numbers consists of:

- Determining what place value the number is being rounded to
- Examining the digit to the right of the desired place value to decide whether to round up or keep the digit
- Replacing all digits to the right of the desired place value with zeros

To round 746,311 to the nearest ten thousands, the digit in the ten thousands place should be located first. In this case, this digit is 4 (7<u>4</u>6,311). Then, the digit to its right is examined. If this digit is 5 or greater, the number will be rounded up by increasing the digit in the desired place by one. If the digit to the right of the place value being rounded is 4 or less, the number will be kept the same. For the given example, the digit being examined is a 6, which means that the number will be rounded up by increasing the digit to the left by one. Therefore, the digit 4 is changed to a 5. Finally, to write the rounded number, any digits to the left of the place value being rounded remain the same and any to its right are replaced with zeros. For the given example, rounding 746,311 to the nearest ten thousand will produce 750,000. To round 746,311 to the nearest hundred, the digit to the right of the three in the hundreds place is examined to determine whether to round up or keep the same number. In this case, that digit is a one, so the number will be kept the same and any digits to its right will be replaced with zeros. The resulting rounded number is 746,300.

Rounding place values to the right of the decimal follows the same procedure, but digits being replaced by zeros can simply be dropped. To round 3.752891 to the nearest thousandth, the desired place value is located (3.75<u>2</u>891) and the digit to the right is examined. In this case, the digit 8 indicates that the number will be rounded up, and the 2 in the thousandths place will increase to a 3. Rounding up and replacing the digits to the right of the thousandths place produces 3.753000 which is equivalent to 3.753. Therefore, the zeros are not necessary and the rounded number should be written as 3.753.

When rounding up, if the digit to be increased is a 9, the digit to its left is increased by 1 and the digit in the desired place value is changed to a zero. For example, the number 1,598 rounded to the nearest ten is 1,600. Another example shows the number 43.72961 rounded to the nearest thousandth is 43.730 or 43.73.

Solving Multistep Mathematical and Real-World Problems

Problem Situations for Operations

Addition and subtraction are *inverse operations*. Adding a number and then subtracting the same number will cancel each other out, resulting in the original number, and vice versa. For example, $8 + 7 - 7 = 8$ and $137 - 100 + 100 = 137$. Similarly, multiplication and division are inverse operations. Therefore, multiplying by a number and then dividing by the same number results in the original number, and vice versa. For example, $8 \times 2 \div 2 = 8$ and $12 \div 4 \times 4 = 12$. Inverse operations are used to work backwards to solve problems. In the case that 7 and a number add to 18, the inverse operation of subtraction is used to find the unknown value ($18 - 7 = 11$). If a school's entire 4th grade was divided evenly into 3 classes each with 22 students, the inverse operation of multiplication is used to determine the total students in the grade ($22 \times 3 = 66$). Additional scenarios involving inverse operations are included in the tables below.

There are a variety of real-world situations in which one or more of the operators is used to solve a problem. The tables below display the most common scenarios.

Addition & Subtraction

	Unknown Result	Unknown Change	Unknown Start
Adding to	5 students were in class. 4 more students arrived. How many students are in class? $5 + 4 =?$	8 students were in class. More students arrived late. There are now 18 students in class. How many students arrived late? $8+? = 18$ Solved by inverse operations $18-8 =?$	Some students were in class early. 11 more students arrived. There are now 17 students in class. How many students were in class early? $? +11 = 17$ Solved by inverse operations $17-11 =?$
Taking from	15 students were in class. 5 students left class. How many students are in class now? $15-5 =?$	12 students were in class. Some students left class. There are now 8 students in class. How many students left class? $12-? = 8$ Solved by inverse operations $8+? = 12 \rightarrow 12-8 =?$	Some students were in class. 3 students left class. Then there were 13 students in class. How many students were in class before? $?-3 = 13$ Solved by inverse operations $13 + 3 =?$

	Unknown Total	Unknown Addends (Both)	Unknown Addends (One)
Putting together/ taking apart	The homework assignment is 10 addition problems and 8 subtraction problems. How many problems are in the homework assignment? $10 + 8 =?$	Bobby has $9. How much can Bobby spend on candy and how much can Bobby spend on toys? $9 =? +?$	Bobby has 12 pairs of pants. 5 pairs of pants are shorts and the rest are long. How many pairs of long pants does he have? $12 = 5+?$ Solved by inverse operations $12-5 =?$

	Unknown Difference	Unknown Larger Value	Unknown Smaller Value
Comparing	Bobby has 5 toys. Tommy has 8 toys. How many more toys does Tommy have than Bobby? $5+?=8$ Solved by inverse operations $8-5=?$ Bobby has $6. Tommy has $10. How many fewer dollars does Bobby have than Tommy? $10-6=?$	Tommy has 2 more toys than Bobby. Bobby has 4 toys. How many toys does Tommy have? $2+4=?$ Bobby has 3 fewer dollars than Tommy. Bobby has $8. How many dollars does Tommy have? $?-3=8$ Solved by inverse operations $8+3=?$	Tommy has 6 more toys than Bobby. Tommy has 10 toys. How many toys does Bobby have? $?+6=10$ Solved by inverse operations $10-6=?$ Bobby has $5 less than Tommy. Tommy has $9. How many dollars does Bobby have? $9-5=?$

Multiplication and Division

	Unknown Product	Unknown Group Size	Unknown Number of Groups
Equal groups	There are 5 students and each student has 4 pieces of candy. How many pieces of candy are there in all? $5\times4=?$	14 pieces of candy are shared equally by 7 students. How many pieces of candy does each student have? $7\times?=14$ Solved by inverse operations $14\div7=?$	If 18 pieces of candy are to be given out 3 to each student, how many students will get candy? $?\times3=18$ Solved by inverse operations $18\div3=?$

	Unknown Product	Unknown Factor	Unknown Factor
Arrays	There are 5 rows of students with 3 students in each row. How many students are there? $5\times3=?$	If 16 students are arranged into 4 equal rows, how many students will be in each row? $4\times?=16$ Solved by inverse operations $16\div4=?$	If 24 students are arranged into an array with 6 columns, how many rows are there? $?\times6=24$ Solved by inverse operations $24\div6=?$

	Larger Unknown	Smaller Unknown	Multiplier Unknown
Comparing	A small popcorn costs $1.50. A large popcorn costs 3 times as much as a small popcorn. How much does a large popcorn cost? $1.50 \times 3 =?$	A large soda costs $6 and that is 2 times as much as a small soda costs. How much does a small soda cost? $2 \times ? = 6$ Solved by inverse operations $6 \div 2 =?$	A large pretzel costs $3 and a small pretzel costs $2. How many times as much does the large pretzel cost as the small pretzel? $? \times 2 = 3$ Solved by inverse operations $3 \div 2 =?$

Remainders in Division Problems

If a given total cannot be divided evenly into a given number of groups, the amount left over is the remainder. Consider the following scenario: 32 textbooks must be packed into boxes for storage. Each box holds 6 textbooks. How many boxes are needed? To determine the answer, 32 is divided by 6, resulting in 5 with a remainder of 2. A remainder may be interpreted three ways:

- Add 1 to the quotient
  How many boxes will be needed? Six boxes will be needed because five will not be enough.

- Use only the quotient
  How many boxes will be full? Five boxes will be full.

- Use only the remainder
  If you only have 5 boxes, how many books will not fit? Two books will not fit.

Strategies and Algorithms to Perform Operations on Rational Numbers

A rational number is any number that can be written in the form of a ratio or fraction. Integers can be written as fractions with a denominator of 1 ($5 = \frac{5}{1}$; $-342 = \frac{-342}{1}$; etc.). Decimals that terminate and/or repeat can also be written as fractions ($47 = \frac{47}{100}$; $.\overline{33} = \frac{1}{3}$). For more on converting decimals to fractions, see the section *Converting Between Fractions, Decimals,* and *Percent*.

When adding or subtracting fractions, the numbers must have the same denominators. In these cases, numerators are added or subtracted and denominators are kept the same. For example, $\frac{2}{7} + \frac{3}{7} = \frac{5}{7}$ and $\frac{4}{5} - \frac{3}{5} = \frac{1}{5}$. If the fractions to be added or subtracted do not have the same denominator, a common denominator must be found. This is accomplished by changing one or both fractions to a different but equivalent fraction. Consider the example $\frac{1}{6} + \frac{4}{9}$. First, a common denominator must be found. One method is to find the least common multiple (LCM) of the denominators 6 and 9. This is the lowest number that both 6 and 9 will divide into evenly. In this case the LCM is 18. Both fractions should be changed to equivalent fractions with a denominator of 18. To obtain the numerator of the new fraction, the old numerator is multiplied by the same number by which the old denominator is multiplied. For the fraction $\frac{1}{6}$, 6 multiplied by 3 will produce a denominator of 18. Therefore, the numerator is multiplied by 3 to produce the new numerator $\left(\frac{1 \times 3}{6 \times 3} = \frac{3}{18}\right)$. For the fraction $\frac{4}{9}$, multiplying both the numerator and denominator by 2 produces $\frac{8}{18}$. Since the two new fractions have common denominators, they can be added $\left(\frac{3}{18} + \frac{8}{18} = \frac{11}{18}\right)$.

When multiplying or dividing rational numbers, these numbers may be converted to fractions and multiplied or divided accordingly. When multiplying fractions, all numerators are multiplied by each other and all denominators are multiplied by each other. For example, $\frac{1}{3} \times \frac{6}{5} = \frac{1 \times 6}{3 \times 5} = \frac{6}{15}$ and $\frac{-1}{2} \times \frac{3}{1} \times \frac{11}{100} = \frac{-1 \times 3 \times 11}{2 \times 1 \times 100} = \frac{-33}{200}$. When dividing fractions, the problem is converted by multiplying by the reciprocal of the divisor. This is done by changing division to multiplication and "flipping" the second fraction, or divisor. For example, $\frac{1}{2} \div \frac{3}{5} \rightarrow \frac{1}{2} \times \frac{5}{3}$ and $\frac{5}{1} \div \frac{1}{3} \rightarrow \frac{5}{1} \times \frac{3}{1}$. To complete the problem, the rules for multiplying fractions should be followed.

Note that when adding, subtracting, multiplying, and dividing mixed numbers (ex. $4\frac{1}{2}$), it is easiest to convert these to improper fractions (larger numerator than denominator). To do so, the denominator is kept the same. To obtain the numerator, the whole number is multiplied by the denominator and added to the numerator. For example, $4\frac{1}{2} = \frac{9}{2}$ and $7\frac{2}{3} = \frac{23}{3}$. Also, note that answers involving fractions should be converted to the simplest form.

Rational Numbers and Their Operations

<u>Irregular Products and Quotients</u>
The following shows examples where multiplication does not result in a product greater than both factors, and where division does not result in a quotient smaller than the dividend.

If multiplying numbers where one or more has a value less than one, the product will not be greater than both factors. For example, $6 \times \frac{1}{2} = 3$ and $0.75 \times 0.2 = .15$. When dividing by a number less than one, the resulting quotient will be greater than the dividend. For example, $8 \div \frac{1}{2} = 16$, because division turns into a multiplication problem, $8 \div \frac{1}{2} \rightarrow 8 \times \frac{2}{1}$. Another example is $0.5 \div 0.2$, which results in 2.5. The problem can be stated by asking how many times 0.2 will go into 0.5. The number being divided is larger than the number that goes into it, so the result will be a number larger than both factors.

<u>Composing and Decomposing Fractions</u>

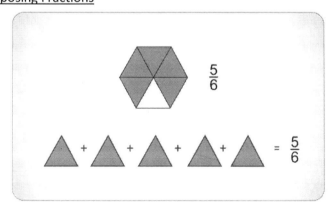

Fractions can be broken apart into sums of fractions with the same denominator. For example, the fraction $\frac{5}{6}$ can be decomposed into sums of fractions with all denominators equal to 6 and the numerators adding to 5. The fraction $\frac{5}{6}$ is decomposed as: $\frac{3}{6} + \frac{2}{6}$; or $\frac{2}{6} + \frac{2}{6} + \frac{1}{6}$; or $\frac{3}{6} + \frac{1}{6} + \frac{1}{6}$; or $\frac{1}{6} + \frac{1}{6} + \frac{1}{6} + \frac{2}{6}$; or $\frac{1}{6} + \frac{1}{6} + \frac{1}{6} + \frac{1}{6} + \frac{1}{6}$.

A unit fraction is a fraction in which the numerator is 1. If decomposing a fraction into unit fractions, the sum will consist of a unit fraction added the number of times equal to the numerator. For example, $\frac{3}{4} = \frac{1}{4} + \frac{1}{4} + \frac{1}{4}$ (unit fractions $\frac{1}{4}$ added 3 times). Composing fractions is simply the opposite of decomposing. It is the process of adding fractions with the same denominators to produce a single fraction. For example, $\frac{3}{7} + \frac{2}{7} = \frac{5}{7}$ and $\frac{1}{5} + \frac{1}{5} + \frac{1}{5} = \frac{3}{5}$.

Decrease in Value of a Unit Fraction

A unit fraction is one in which the numerator is 1 ($\frac{1}{2}, \frac{1}{3}, \frac{1}{8}, \frac{1}{20}$, etc.). The denominator indicates the number of *equal pieces* that the whole is divided into. The greater the number of pieces, the smaller each piece will be. Therefore, the greater the denominator of a unit fraction, the smaller it is in value. Unit fractions can also be compared by converting them to decimals. For example, $\frac{1}{2} = 0.5, \frac{1}{3} = 0.\bar{3}, \frac{1}{8} = 0.125, \frac{1}{20} = 0.05$, etc.

Use of the Same Whole when Comparing Fractions

Fractions all represent parts of the same whole. Fractions may have different denominators, but they represent parts of the same one whole, like a pizza. For example, the fractions $\frac{5}{7}$ and $\frac{2}{3}$ can be difficult to compare because they have different denominators. The first fraction may represent a whole divided into seven parts, where five parts are used. The second fraction represents the same whole divided into three parts, where two are used. It may be helpful to convert one or more of the fractions so that they have common denominators for converting to equivalent fractions by finding the LCM of the denominator. Comparing is much easier if fractions are converted to the equivalent fractions of $\frac{15}{21}$ and $\frac{14}{21}$. These fractions show a whole divided into 21 parts, where the numerators can be compared because the denominators are the same.

Order of Operations

When reviewing calculations consisting of more than one operation, the order in which the operations are performed affects the resulting answer. Consider $5 \times 2 + 7$. Performing multiplication then addition results in an answer of 17 ($5 \times 2 = 10$; $10 + 7 = 17$). However, if the problem is written $5 \times (2 + 7)$, the order of operations dictates that the operation inside the parenthesis must be performed first. The resulting answer is 45 ($2 + 7 = 9$, then $5 \times 9 = 45$).

The order in which operations should be performed is remembered using the acronym PEMDAS. PEMDAS stands for parenthesis, exponents, multiplication/division, and addition/subtraction. Multiplication and division are performed in the same step, working from left to right with whichever comes first. Addition and subtraction are performed in the same step, working from left to right with whichever comes first.

Consider the following example: $8 \div 4 + 8(7 - 7)$. Performing the operation inside the parenthesis produces $8 \div 4 + 8(0)$ or $8 \div 4 + 8 \times 0$. There are no exponents, so multiplication and division are performed next from left to right resulting in: $2 + 8 \times 0$, then $2 + 0$. Finally, addition and subtraction are performed to obtain an answer of 2. Now consider the following example: $6 \times 3 + 3^2 - 6$. Parentheses are not applicable. Exponents are evaluated first, $6 \times 3 + 9 - 6$. Then multiplication/division forms $18 + 9 - 6$. At last, addition/subtraction leads to the final answer of 21.

Properties of Operations

Properties of operations exist that make calculations easier and solve problems for missing values. The following table summarizes commonly used properties of real numbers.

Property	Addition	Multiplication
Commutative	$a + b = b + a$	$a \times b = b \times a$
Associative	$(a + b) + c = a + (b + c)$	$(a \times b) \times c = a \times (bc)$
Identity	$a + 0 = a; 0 + a = a$	$a \times 1 = a; 1 \times a = a$
Inverse	$a + (-a) = 0$	$a \times \frac{1}{a} = 1; a \neq 0$
Distributive	$a(b + c) = ab + ac$	

The commutative property of addition states that the order in which numbers are added does not change the sum. Similarly, the commutative property of multiplication states that the order in which numbers are multiplied does not change the product. The associative property of addition and multiplication state that the grouping of numbers being added or multiplied does not change the sum or product, respectively. The commutative and associative properties are useful for performing calculations. For example, $(47 + 25) + 3$ is equivalent to $(47 + 3) + 25$, which is easier to calculate.

The identity property of addition states that adding zero to any number does not change its value. The identity property of multiplication states that multiplying a number by one does not change its value. The inverse property of addition states that the sum of a number and its opposite equals zero. Opposites are numbers that are the same with different signs (ex. 5 and -5; $-\frac{1}{2}$ and $\frac{1}{2}$). The inverse property of multiplication states that the product of a number (other than zero) and its reciprocal equals one. Reciprocal numbers have numerators and denominators that are inverted (ex. $\frac{2}{5}$ and $\frac{5}{2}$). Inverse properties are useful for canceling quantities to find missing values (see algebra content). For example, $a + 7 = 12$ is solved by adding the inverse of 7(-7) to both sides in order to isolate a.

The distributive property states that multiplying a sum (or difference) by a number produces the same result as multiplying each value in the sum (or difference) by the number and adding (or subtracting) the products. Consider the following scenario: You are buying three tickets for a baseball game. Each ticket costs $18. You are also charged a fee of $2 per ticket for purchasing the tickets online. The cost is calculated: $3 \times 18 + 3 \times 2$. Using the distributive property, the cost can also be calculated $3(18 + 2)$.

Representing Rational Numbers and Their Operations

Concrete Models

Concrete objects are used to develop a tangible understanding of operations of rational numbers. Tools such as tiles, blocks, beads, and hundred charts are used to model problems. For example, a hundred chart (10×10) and beads can be used to model multiplication. If multiplying 5 by 4, beads are placed across 5 rows and down 4 columns producing a product of 20. Similarly, tiles can be used to model division by splitting the total into equal groups. If dividing 12 by 4, 12 tiles are placed one at a time into 4 groups. The result is 4 groups of 3. This is also an effective method for visualizing the concept of remainders.

Representations of objects can be used to expand on the concrete models of operations. Pictures, dots, and tallies can help model these concepts. Utilizing concrete models and representations creates a foundation upon which to build an abstract understanding of the operations.

Rational Numbers on a Number Line

A number line typically consists of integers (...3,2,1,0,-1,-2,-3...), and is used to visually represent the value of a rational number. Each rational number has a distinct position on the line determined by comparing its value with the displayed values on the line. For example, if plotting -1.5 on the number line below, it is necessary to recognize that the value of -1.5 is .5 less than -1 and .5 greater than -2. Therefore, -1.5 is plotted halfway between -1 and -2.

Number lines can also be useful for visualizing sums and differences of rational numbers. Adding a value indicates moving to the right (values increase to the right), and subtracting a value indicates moving to the left (numbers decrease to the left). For example, $5 - 7$ is displayed by starting at 5 and moving to the left 7 spaces, if the number line is in increments of 1. This will result in an answer of -2.

Multiplication and Division Problems

Multiplication and division are inverse operations that can be represented by using rectangular arrays, area models, and equations. Rectangular arrays include an arrangement of rows and columns that correspond to the factors and display product totals.

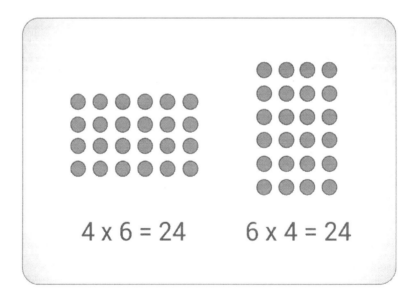

Another method of multiplication can be done with the use of an *area model*. An area model is a rectangle that is divided into rows and columns that match up to the number of place values within each number. For example, $29 \times 65 = 25 + 4$ and $65 = 60 + 5$. The products of those 4 numbers are found within the rectangle and then summed up to get the answer. The entire process is: $(60 \times 25) + (5 \times 25) + (60 \times 4) + (5 \times 4) = 1,500 + 240 + 125 + 20 = 1,885$. Here is the actual area model:

	25	**4**
60	60x25 1,500	60x4 240
5	5x25 125	5x4 20

$$
\begin{array}{r}
1,500 \\
240 \\
125 \\
+\quad 20 \\
\hline
1,885
\end{array}
$$

Multiplying decimals involves the same procedure as multiplying whole numbers, but including the decimal places in the end result. The problem involves multiplying the two numbers together, ignoring the decimal places, and then inserting the total number of decimal places in the original numbers into the result. For example, given the problem 87.5×0.45, the answer is found by multiplying 875×45 to obtain 39,375 and then inputting a decimal point three places to the left because there are three total decimal places in the original problem. Therefore, the answer is 39.375.

Dividing a number by a single digit or two digits can be turned into repeated subtraction problems. An area model can be used throughout the problem that represents multiples of the divisor. For example, the answer to $8580 \div 55$ can be found by subtracting 55 from 8580 one at a time and counting the total number of subtractions necessary.

However, a simpler process involves using larger multiples of 55. First, $100 \times 55 = 5,500$ is subtracted from 8,580, and 3,080 is leftover. Next, $50 \times 55 = 2,750$ is subtracted from 3,080 to obtain380. $5 \times 55 = 275$ is subtracted from 330 to obtain 55, and finally, $1 \times 55 = 55$ is subtracted from 55 to obtain zero. Therefore, there is no remainder, and the answer is $100 + 50 + 5 + 1 = 156$. Here is a picture of the area model and the repeated subtraction process:

$$8580 \div 55$$

$$
\begin{array}{c|c}
 & 55 \\
100 & 5500 \\
50 & 2750 \\
5 & 275 \\
1 & 55 \\
\end{array}
$$

$$
\begin{array}{r}
55\overline{)8580} \\
-5500 \quad (100 \times 55) \\
\hline
3080 \\
-2750 \quad (50 \times 55) \\
\hline
330 \\
-275 \quad (5 \times 55) \\
\hline
55 \\
-55 \quad (1 \times 55) \\
\hline
0 \\
\end{array}
$$

Checking the answer to a division problem involves multiplying the answer—the quotient—times the divisor to see if the dividend is obtained. If there is a remainder, the same process is computed, but the remainder is added on at the end to try to match the dividend. In the previous example, $156 \times 55 = 8580$ would be the checking procedure. Dividing decimals involves the same repeated subtraction process. The only difference would be that the subtractions would involve numbers that include values in the decimal places. Lining up decimal places is crucial in this type of problem.

Comparing, Classifying, and Ordering Rational Numbers

Rational numbers are any number that can be written as a fraction or ratio. Within the set of rational numbers, several subsets exist that are referenced throughout the mathematics topics. Counting numbers are the first numbers learned as a child. Counting numbers consist of 1,2,3,4, and so on. Whole numbers include all counting numbers and zero (0,1,2,3,4,...). Integers include counting numbers, their opposites, and zero (...,-3,-2,-1,0,1,2,3,...). Rational numbers are inclusive of integers, fractions, and decimals that terminate, or end (1.7, 0.04213) or repeat ($0.136\overline{5}$).

When comparing or ordering numbers, the numbers should be written in the same format (decimal or fraction), if possible. For example, $\sqrt{49}$, 7.3, and $\frac{15}{2}$ are easier to order if each one is converted to a decimal, such as 7, 7.3, and 7.5 (converting fractions and decimals is covered in the following section). A number line is used to order and compare the numbers. Any number that is to the right of another number is greater than that number. Conversely, a number positioned to the left of a given number is less than that number.

Converting Between Fractions, Decimals, and Percent

To convert a fraction to a decimal, the numerator is divided by the denominator. For example, $\frac{3}{8}$ can be converted to a decimal by dividing 3 by 8 ($\frac{3}{8} = 0.375$). To convert a decimal to a fraction, the decimal point is dropped and the value is written as the numerator. The denominator is the place value farthest to the right with a digit other than zero. For example, to convert .48 to a fraction, the numerator is 48 and the denominator is 100 (the digit 8 is in the hundredths place). Therefore, $.48 = \frac{48}{100}$. Fractions should be written in the simplest form, or reduced. To reduce a fraction, the numerator and denominator are divided by the largest common factor. In the previous example, 48 and 100 are both divisible by 4. Dividing the numerator and denominator by 4 results in a reduced fraction of $\frac{12}{25}$.

To convert a decimal to a percent, the number is multiplied by 100. To convert .13 to a percent, .13 is multiplied by 100 to get 13 percent. To convert a fraction to a percent, the fraction is converted to a decimal and then multiplied by 100. For example, $\frac{1}{5}$ = .20 and .20 multiplied by 100 produces 20 percent.

To convert a percent to a decimal, the value is divided by 100. For example, 125 percent is equal to 1.25 $(\frac{125}{100})$. To convert a percent to a fraction, the percent sign is dropped and the value is written as the numerator with a denominator of 100. For example, $80\% = \frac{80}{100}$. This fraction can be reduced $(\frac{80}{100} = \frac{4}{5})$.

Understanding Proportional Relationships and Percent

Applying Ratios and Unit Rates

A ratio is a comparison of two quantities that represent separate groups. For example, if a recipe calls for 2 eggs for every 3 cups of milk, this is expressed as a ratio. Ratios can be written three ways:

- With the word "to"
- Using a colon
- As a fraction.

In the previous example, the ratio of eggs to cups of milk is written as 2 to 3, 2:3, or $\frac{2}{3}$. When writing ratios, the order is very important. The ratio of eggs to cups of milk is not the same as the ratio of cups of milk to eggs, 3:2.

In simplest form, both quantities of a ratio should be written as integers. These should also be reduced just as a fraction is reduced. For example, 5:10 is reduced to 1:2. Given a ratio where one or both quantities are expressed as a decimal or fraction, multiply both by the same number to produce integers. To write the ratio $\frac{1}{3}$ to 2 in simplest form, both quantities are multiplied by 3. The resulting ratio is 1 to 6.

A problem involving ratios may give a comparison between two groups. The problem may then provide a total and ask for a part, or provide a part and ask for a total. Consider the following: The ratio of boys to girls in the 11th grade class is 5:4. If there are a total of 270 11th grade students, how many are girls? The total number of *ratio pieces* should be determined first. The total number of 11th grade students is divided into 9 pieces. The ratio of boys to total students is 5:9, and the ratio of girls to total students is 4:9. Knowing the total number of students, the number of girls is determined by setting up a proportion: $\frac{4}{9} = \frac{x}{270}$.

A rate is a ratio comparing two quantities expressed in different units. A unit rate is a ratio in which the second quantity is one unit. Rates often include the word *per*. Examples include miles per hour, beats per minute, and price per pound. The word per is represented with a / symbol or abbreviated with the letter *p* and units abbreviated. For example, miles per hour is written as mi/h. When given a rate that is not in its simplest form (the second quantity is not one unit), both quantities are divided by the value of the second quantity. If 99 heartbeats were recorded in $1\frac{1}{2}$ minutes, both quantities are divided by $1\frac{1}{2}$ to determine the heart rate of 66 beats per minute.

Percent

The word percent means per hundred. Similar to a unit rate in which the second quantity is always one unit, a percent is a rate where the second quantity is always 100 units. If the results of a poll state that 47 percent of people support a given policy, this indicates that 47 out of every 100 individuals polled were in support. In other words, 47 per 100 support the policy. If an upgraded model of a car costs 110 percent of the cost of the base model, for every $100 that is spent for the base model, $110 must be spent to purchase the upgraded model. In other words, the upgraded model costs $110 per $100 for the cost of the base model.

When dealing with percentages, the numbers can be evaluated as a value in hundredths. For example, 15 percent is expressed as fifteen hundredths and is written as $\frac{15}{100}$ or 0.15.

Unit-Rate Problems

A rate is a ratio in which two terms are in different units. When rates are expressed as a quantity of one, they are considered unit rates. To determine a unit rate, the first quantity is divided by the second. Knowing a unit rate makes calculations easier than simply having a rate. For example, suppose a 3 pound bag of onions costs $1.77. To calculate the price of 5 pounds of onions, a proportion could show: $\frac{3}{1.77} = \frac{5}{x}$. However, by knowing the unit rate, the value of pounds of onions is multiplied by the unit price. The unit price is calculated: $\$1.77/3lb = \$0.59/lb$. Multiplying the weight of the onions by the unit price yields: $5lb \times \frac{\$0.59}{lb} = \$2.95$. The *lb.* units cancel out.

Similar to unit-rate problems, unit conversions appear in real-world scenarios including cooking, measurement, construction, and currency. Given the conversion rate, unit conversions are written as a fraction (ratio) and multiplied by a quantity in one unit to convert it to the corresponding unit. To determine how many minutes are in $3\frac{1}{2}$ hours, the conversion rate of 60 minutes to 1 hour is written as $\frac{60\ min}{1h}$. Multiplying the quantity by the conversion rate results in $3\frac{1}{2}h \times \frac{60\ min}{1h} = 210\ min$. (The h unit is canceled.) To convert a quantity in minutes to hours, the fraction for the conversion rate is flipped to cancel the *min* unit. To convert 195 minutes to hours, $195min \times \frac{1h}{60\ min}$ is multiplied. The result is $\frac{195h}{60}$ which reduces to $3\frac{1}{4}h$.

Converting units may require more than one multiplication. The key is to set up conversion rates so that units cancel each other out and the desired unit is left. To convert 3.25 yards to inches, given that 1yd = 3ft and 12in = 1ft, the calculation is performed by multiplying $3.25\ yd \times \frac{3ft}{1yd} \times \frac{12in}{1ft}$. The yd and ft units will cancel, resulting in 117in.

Using Proportional Relationships

A proportion is a statement consisting of two equal ratios. Proportions will typically give three of four quantities and require solving for the missing value. The key to solving proportions is to set them up properly. Consider the following: 7 gallons of gas costs $14.70. How many gallons can you get for $20? The information is written as equal ratios with a variable representing the missing quantity $\left(\frac{gallons}{cost} = \frac{gallons}{cost}\right): \frac{7}{14.70} = \frac{x}{20}$. To solve for x, the proportion is cross-multiplied. This means the numerator of the first ratio is multiplied by the denominator of the second, and vice versa. The resulting products are shown equal to each other. Cross-multiplying results in $(7)(20) = (14.7)(x)$. By solving the equation for x (see the algebra content), the answer is that 9.5 gallons of gas may be purchased for $20.

Percent problems can also be solved by setting up proportions. Examples of common percent problems are:

    a. What is 15% of 25?
    b. What percent of 45 is 3?
    c. 5 is $\frac{1}{2}$% of what number?

Setting up the proper proportion is made easier by following the format: $\frac{is}{of} = \frac{percent}{100}$. A variable is used to represent the missing value. The proportions for each of the three examples are set up as follows:

    a. $\dfrac{x}{25} = \dfrac{15}{100}$
    b. $\dfrac{3}{45} = \dfrac{x}{100}$
    c. $\dfrac{5}{x} = \dfrac{\frac{1}{2}}{100}$

By cross-multiplying and solving the resulting equation for the variable, the missing values are determined to be:

    a. 3.75
    b. $6.\bar{6}$%
    c. 1,000

Basic Concepts of Number Theory

Prime and Composite Numbers
Whole numbers are classified as either prime or composite. A prime number can only be divided evenly by itself and one. For example, the number 11 can only be divided evenly by 11 and one; therefore, 11 is a prime number. A helpful way to visualize a prime number is to use concrete objects and try to divide them into equal piles. If dividing 11 coins, the only way to divide them into equal piles is to create 1 pile of 11 coins or to create 11 piles of 1 coin each. Other examples of prime numbers include 2, 3, 5, 7, 13, 17, and 19.

A composite number is any whole number that is not a prime number. A composite number is a number that can be divided evenly by one or more numbers other than itself and one. For example, the number 6 can be divided evenly by 2 and 3. Therefore, 6 is a composite number. If dividing 6 coins into equal piles, the possibilities are 1 pile of 6 coins, 2 piles of 3 coins, 3 piles of 2 coins, or 6 piles of 1 coin. Other examples of composite numbers include 4, 8, 9, 10, 12, 14, 15, 16, 18, and 20.

To determine if a number is a prime or composite number, the number is divided by every whole number greater than one and less than its own value. If it divides evenly by any of these numbers, then the number is composite. If it does not divide evenly by any of these numbers, then the number is prime. For example, when attempting to divide the number 5 by 2, 3, and 4, none of these numbers divide evenly. Therefore, 5 must be a prime number.

Factors and Multiples of Numbers

The factors of a number are all integers that can be multiplied by another integer to produce the given number. For example, 2 is multiplied by 3 to produce 6. Therefore, 2 and 3 are both factors of 6. Similarly, $1 \times 6 = 6$ and $2 \times 3 = 6$, so 1, 2, 3, and 6 are all factors of 6. Another way to explain a factor is to say that a given number divides evenly by each of its factors to produce an integer. For example, 6 does not divide evenly by 5. Therefore, 5 is not a factor of 6.

Multiples of a given number are found by taking that number and multiplying it by any other whole number. For example, 3 is a factor of 6, 9, and 12. Therefore, 6, 9, and 12 are multiples of 3. The multiples of any number are an infinite list. For example, the multiples of 5 are 5, 10, 15, 20, and so on. This list continues without end. A list of multiples is used in finding the least common multiple, or LCM, for fractions when a common denominator is needed. The denominators are written down and their multiples listed until a common number is found in both lists. This common number is the LCM.

Prime factorization breaks down each factor of a whole number until only prime numbers remain. All composite numbers can be factored into prime numbers. For example, the prime factors of 12 are 2, 2, and 3 ($2 \times 2 \times 3 = 12$). To produce the prime factors of a number, the number is factored and any composite numbers are continuously factored until the result is the product of prime factors only. A factor tree, such as the one below, is helpful when exploring this concept.

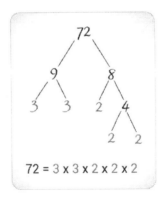

$72 = 3 \times 3 \times 2 \times 2 \times 2$

Determining the Reasonableness of Results

When solving math word problems, the solution obtained should make sense within the given scenario. The step of checking the solution will reduce the possibility of a calculation error or a solution that may be *mathematically* correct but not applicable in the real world. Consider the following scenarios:

A problem states that Lisa got 24 out of 32 questions correct on a test and asks to find the percentage of correct answers. To solve the problem, a student divided 32 by 24 to get 1.33, and then multiplied by 100 to get 133 percent. By examining the solution within the context of the problem, the student should recognize that getting all 32 questions correct will produce a perfect score of 100 percent. Therefore, a score of 133 percent with 8 incorrect answers does not make sense and the calculations should be checked.

A problem states that the maximum weight on a bridge cannot exceed 22,000 pounds. The problem asks to find the maximum number of cars that can be on the bridge at one time if each car weighs 4,000 pounds. To solve this problem, a student divided 22,000 by 4,000 to get an answer of 5.5. By examining the solution within the context of the problem, the student should recognize that although the calculations are mathematically correct, the solution does not make sense. Half of a car on a bridge is not possible, so the student should determine that a maximum of 5 cars can be on the bridge at the same time.

Mental Math Estimation

Once a result is determined to be logical within the context of a given problem, the result should be evaluated by its nearness to the expected answer. This is performed by approximating given values to perform mental math. Numbers should be rounded to the nearest value possible to check the initial results.

Consider the following example: A problem states that a customer is buying a new sound system for their home. The customer purchases a stereo for $435, 2 speakers for $67 each, and the necessary cables for $12. The customer chooses an option that allows him to spread the costs over equal payments for 4 months. How much will the monthly payments be?

After making calculations for the problem, a student determines that the monthly payment will be $145.25. To check the accuracy of the results, the student rounds each cost to the nearest ten ($440 + 70 + 70 + 10$) and determines that the total is approximately $590. Dividing by 4 months gives an approximate monthly payment of $147.50. Therefore, the student can conclude that the solution of $145.25 is very close to what should be expected.

When rounding, the place-value that is used in rounding can make a difference. Suppose the student had rounded to the nearest hundred for the estimation. The result ($400 + 100 + 100 + 0 = 600; 600 \div 4 = 150$) will show that the answer is reasonable, but not as close to the actual value as rounding to the nearest ten.

Algebra

Algebraic Expressions and Equations

An algebraic expression is a statement about an unknown quantity expressed in mathematical symbols. A variable is used to represent the unknown quantity, usually denoted by a letter. An equation is a statement in which two expressions (at least one containing a variable) are equal to each other. An algebraic expression can be thought of as a mathematical phrase and an equation can be thought of as a mathematical sentence.

Algebraic expressions and equations both contain numbers, variables, and mathematical operations. The following are examples of algebraic expressions: $5x + 3, 7xy - 8(x^2 + y)$, and $\sqrt{a^2 + b^2}$. An expression can be simplified or evaluated for given values of variables. The following are examples of equations: $2x + 3 = 7, a^2 + b^2 = c^2$, and $2x + 5 = 3x - 2$. An equation contains two sides separated by an equal sign. Equations can be solved to determine the value(s) of the variable for which the statement is true.

Adding and Subtracting Linear Algebraic Expressions

An algebraic expression is simplified by combining like terms. A term is a number, variable, or product of a number, and variables separated by addition and subtraction. For the algebraic expression $3x^2 - 4x + 5 - 5x^2 + x - 3$, the terms are $3x^2$, -4x, 5, -5x^2, x, and -3. Like terms have the same variables raised to the same powers (exponents). The like terms for the previous example are $3x^2$ and -5x^2, -4x and x, 5 and -3. To combine like terms, the coefficients (numerical factor of the term including sign) are added

43

and the variables and their powers are kept the same. Note that if a coefficient is not written, it is an implied coefficient of 1 ($x = 1x$). The previous example will simplify to $-2x^2 - 3x + 2$.

When adding or subtracting algebraic expressions, each expression is written in parenthesis. The negative sign is distributed when necessary, and like terms are combined. Consider the following: add $2a + 5b - 2$ to $a - 2b + 8c - 4$. The sum is set as follows: $(a - 2b + 8c - 4) + (2a + 5b - 2)$. In front of each set of parenthesis is an implied positive one, which, when distributed, does not change any of the terms. Therefore, the parentheses are dropped and like terms are combined: $a - 2b + 8c - 4 + 2a + 5b - 2 = 3a + 3b + 8c - 6$.

Consider the following problem: Subtract $2a + 5b - 2$ from $a - 2b + 8c - 4$. The difference is set as follows: $(a - 2b + 8c - 4) - (2a + 5b - 2)$. The implied one in front of the first set of parenthesis will not change those four terms. However, distributing the implied -1 in front of the second set of parenthesis will change the sign of each of those three terms: $a - 2b + 8c - 4 - 2a - 5b + 2$. Combining like terms yields the simplified expression $-a - 7b + 8c - 2$.

Distributive Property

The distributive property states that multiplying a sum (or difference) by a number produces the same result as multiplying each value in the sum (or difference) by the number and adding (or subtracting) the products. Using mathematical symbols, the distributive property states $a(b + c) = ab + ac$. The expression $4(3 + 2)$ is simplified using the order of operations. Simplifying inside the parenthesis first produces 4×5, which equals 20. The expression $4(3 + 2)$ can also be simplified using the distributive property: $4(3 + 2) = 4 \times 3 + 4 \times 2 = 12 + 8 = 20$.

Consider the following example: $4(3x - 2)$. The expression cannot be simplified inside the parenthesis because $3x$ and -2 are not like terms, and therefore cannot be combined. However, the expression can be simplified by using the distributive property and multiplying each term inside of the parenthesis by the term outside of the parenthesis: $12x - 8$. The resulting equivalent expression contains no like terms, so it cannot be further simplified.

Consider the expression $(3x + 2y + 1) - (5x - 3) + 2(3y + 4)$. Again, there are no like terms, but the distributive property is used to simplify the expression. Note there is an implied one in front of the first set of parentheses and an implied -1 in front of the second set of parentheses. Distributing the one, -1, and 2 produces $1(3x) + 1(2y) + 1(1) - 1(5x) - 1(-3) + 2(3y) + 2(4) = 3x + 2y + 1 - 5x + 3 + 6y + 8$. This expression contains like terms that are combined to produce the simplified expression $-2x + 8y + 12$.

Algebraic expressions are tested to be equivalent by choosing values for the variables and evaluating both expressions (see 2.A.4). For example, $4(3x - 2)$ and $12x - 8$ are tested by substituting 3 for the variable x and calculating to determine if equivalent values result.

Simple Expressions for Given Values

An algebraic expression is a statement written in mathematical symbols, typically including one or more unknown values represented by variables. For example, the expression $2x + 3$ states that an unknown number (x) is multiplied by 2 and added to 3. If given a value for the unknown number, or variable, the value of the expression is determined. For example, if the value of the variable x is 4, the value of the expression 4 is multiplied by 2, and 3 is added. This results in a value of 11 for the expression.

When given an algebraic expression and values for the variable(s), the expression is evaluated to determine its numerical value. To evaluate the expression, the given values for the variables are substituted (or replaced) and the expression is simplified using the order of operations. Parenthesis should be used when substituting. Consider the following: Evaluate $a - 2b + ab$ for $a = 3$ and $b = -1$. To evaluate, any variable a is replaced with 3 and any variable b with -1, producing (3)-2(-1)+(3)(-1). Next, the order of operations is used to calculate the value of the expression, which is 2.

Parts of Expressions

Algebraic expressions consist of variables, numbers, and operations. A term of an expression is any combination of numbers and/or variables, and terms are separated by addition and subtraction. For example, the expression $5x^2 - 3xy + 4 - 2$ consists of 4 terms: $5x^2$, -3xy, 4y, and -2. Note that each term includes its given sign (+ or −). The variable part of a term is a letter that represents an unknown quantity. The coefficient of a term is the number by which the variable is multiplied. For the term 4y, the variable is y and the coefficient is 4. Terms are identified by the power (or exponent) of its variable.

A number without a variable is referred to as a constant. If the variable is to the first power (x^1 or simply x), it is referred to as a linear term. A term with a variable to the second power (x^2) is quadratic and a term to the third power (x^3) is cubic. Consider the expression $x^3 + 3x - 1$. The constant is -1. The linear term is 3x. There is no quadratic term. The cubic term is x^3.

An algebraic expression can also be classified by how many terms exist in the expression. Any like terms should be combined before classifying. A monomial is an expression consisting of only one term. Examples of monomials are: 17, 2x, and $-5ab^2$. A binomial is an expression consisting of two terms separated by addition or subtraction. Examples include $2x - 4$ and $-3y^2 + 2y$. A trinomial consists of 3 terms. For example, $5x^2 - 2x + 1$ is a trinomial.

Verbal Statements and Algebraic Expressions

An algebraic expression is a statement about unknown quantities expressed in mathematical symbols. The statement *five times a number added to forty* is expressed as $5x + 40$. An equation is a statement in which two expressions (with at least one containing a variable) are equal to one another. The statement *five times a number added to forty is equal to ten* is expressed as $5x + 40 = 10$.

Real world scenarios can also be expressed mathematically. Suppose a job pays its employees $300 per week and $40 for each sale made. The weekly pay is represented by the expression $40x + 300$ where x is the number of sales made during the week.

Consider the following scenario: Bob had $20 and Tom had $4. After selling 4 ice cream cones to Bob, Tom has as much money as Bob. The cost of an ice cream cone is an unknown quantity and can be represented by a variable (x). The amount of money Bob has after his purchase is four times the cost of an ice cream cone subtracted from his original $20 $\rightarrow 20 - 4x$. The amount of money Tom has after his sale is four times the cost of an ice cream cone added to his original $4 $\rightarrow 4x + 4$. After the sale, the amount of money that Bob and Tom have are equal $\rightarrow 20 - 4x = 4x + 4$.

When expressing a verbal or written statement mathematically, it is vital to understand words or phrases that can be represented with symbols. The following are examples:

Symbol	Phrase
+	Added to; increased by; sum of; more than
−	Decreased by; difference between; less than; take away
×	Multiplied by; 3(4,5...) times as large; product of
÷	Divided by; quotient of; half (third, etc.) of
=	Is; the same as; results in; as much as; equal to
x,t,n, etc.	A number; unknown quantity; value of; variable

Use of Formulas

Formulas are mathematical expressions that define the value of one quantity, given the value of one or more different quantities. Formulas look like equations because they contain variables, numbers, operators, and an equal sign. All formulas are equations but not all equations are formulas. A formula must have more than one variable. For example, $2x + 7 = y$ is an equation and a formula (it relates the unknown quantities x and y). However, $2x + 7 = 3$ is an equation but not a formula (it only expresses the value of the unknown quantity x).

Formulas are typically written with one variable alone (or isolated) on one side of the equal sign. This variable can be thought of as the *subject* in that the formula is stating the value of the *subject* in terms of the relationship between the other variables. Consider the distance formula: $distance = rate \times time$ or $d = rt$. The value of the subject variable d (distance) is the product of the variable r and t (rate and time). Given the rate and time, the distance traveled can easily be determined by substituting the values into the formula and evaluating.

The formula $P = 2l + 2w$ expresses how to calculate the perimeter of a rectangle (P) given its length (l) and width (w). To find the perimeter of a rectangle with a length of 3ft and a width of 2ft, these values are substituted into the formula for l and w: $P = 2(3ft) + 2(2ft)$. Following the order of operations, the perimeter is determined to be 10ft. When working with formulas such as these, including units is an important step.

Given a formula expressed in terms of one variable, the formula can be manipulated to express the relationship in terms of any other variable. In other words, the formula can be rearranged to change which variable is the *subject*. To solve for a variable of interest by manipulating a formula, the equation may be solved as if all other variables were numbers. The same steps for solving are followed, leaving operations in terms of the variables instead of calculating numerical values. For the formula $P = 2l + 2w$, the perimeter is the subject expressed in terms of the length and width. To write a formula to calculate the width of a rectangle, given its length and perimeter, the previous formula relating the three variables is solved for the variable w. If P and l were numerical values, this is a two-step linear equation solved by subtraction and division. To solve the equation $P = 2l + 2w$ for w, $2l$ is first subtracted from both sides: $P - 2l = 2w$. Then both sides are divided by 2: $\frac{P-2l}{2} = w$.

Dependent and Independent Variables
A variable represents an unknown quantity and, in the case of a formula, a specific relationship exists between the variables. Within a given scenario, variables are the quantities that are changing. If two variables exist, one is dependent and one is independent. The value of one variable depends on the other variable. If a scenario describes distance traveled and time traveled at a given speed, distance is dependent and time is independent. The distance traveled depends on the time spent traveling. If a scenario describes the cost of a cab ride and the distance traveled, the cost is dependent and the

distance is independent. The cost of a cab ride depends on the distance travelled. Formulas often contain more than two variables and are typically written with the dependent variable alone on one side of the equation. This lone variable is the *subject* of the statement. If a formula contains three or more variables, one variable is dependent and the rest are independent. The values of all independent variables are needed to determine the value of the dependent variable.

The formula $P = 2l + 2w$ expresses the dependent variable P in terms of the independent variables, l and w. The perimeter of a rectangle depends on its length and width. The formula $d = rt$ ($distance = rate \times time$) expresses the dependent variable d in terms of the independent variables, r and t. The distance traveled depends on the rate (or speed) and the time traveled.

Multistep One-Variable Linear Equations and Inequalities

Linear equations and linear inequalities are both comparisons of two algebraic expressions. However, unlike equations in which the expressions are equal, linear inequalities compare expressions that may be unequal. Linear equations typically have one value for the variable that makes the statement true. Linear inequalities generally have an infinite number of values that make the statement true.

When solving a linear equation, the desired result requires determining a numerical value for the unknown variable. If given a linear equation involving addition, subtraction, multiplication, or division, working backwards isolates the variable. Addition and subtraction are inverse operations, as are multiplication and division. Therefore, they can be used to cancel each other out.

The first steps to solving linear equations are distributing, if necessary, and combining any like terms on the same side of the equation. Sides of an equation are separated by an *equal* sign. Next, the equation is manipulated to show the variable on one side. Whatever is done to one side of the equation must be done to the other side of the equation to remain equal. Inverse operations are then used to isolate the variable and undo the order of operations backwards. Addition and subtraction are undone, then multiplication and division are undone.

For example, solve $4(t - 2) + 2t - 4 = 2(9 - 2t)$

Distributing: $4t - 8 + 2t - 4 = 18 - 4t$

Combining like terms: $6t - 12 = 18 - 4t$

Adding $4t$ to each side to move the variable: $10t - 12 = 18$

Adding 12 to each side to isolate the variable: $10t = 30$

Dividing each side by 10 to isolate the variable: $t = 3$

The answer can be checked by substituting the value for the variable into the original equation, ensuring that both sides calculate to be equal.

Linear inequalities express the relationship between unequal values. More specifically, they describe in what way the values are unequal. A value can be greater than (>), less than (<), greater than or equal to (≥), or less than or equal to (≤) another value. $5x + 40 > 65$ is read as *five times a number added to forty is greater than sixty-five.*

When solving a linear inequality, the solution is the set of all numbers that make the statement true. The inequality $x + 2 \geq 6$ has a solution set of 4 and every number greater than 4 (4.01; 5; 12; 107; etc.). Adding 2 to 4 or any number greater than 4 results in a value that is greater than or equal to 6. Therefore, $x \geq 4$ is the solution set.

To algebraically solve a linear inequality, follow the same steps as those for solving a linear equation. The inequality symbol stays the same for all operations *except* when multiplying or dividing by a negative number. If multiplying or dividing by a negative number while solving an inequality, the relationship reverses (the sign flips). In other words, > switches to < and vice versa. Multiplying or dividing by a positive number does not change the relationship, so the sign stays the same. An example is shown below.

Solve $-2x - 8 \leq 22$

Add 8 to both sides: $-2x \leq 30$

Divide both sides by -2: $x \geq -15$

Solutions of a linear equation or a linear inequality are the values of the variable that make a statement true. In the case of a linear equation, the solution set (list of all possible solutions) typically consists of a single numerical value. To find the solution, the equation is solved by isolating the variable. For example, solving the equation $3x - 7 = -13$ produces the solution $x = -2$. The only value for x which produces a true statement is -2. This can be checked by substituting -2 into the original equation to check that both sides are equal. In this case, $3(-2) - 7 = -13 \rightarrow -13 = -13$; therefore, -2 is a solution.

Although linear equations generally have one solution, this is not always the case. If there is no value for the variable that makes the statement true, there is no solution to the equation. Consider the equation $x + 3 = x - 1$. There is no value for x in which adding 3 to the value produces the same result as subtracting one from the value. Conversely, if any value for the variable makes a true statement, the equation has an infinite number of solutions. Consider the equation $3x + 6 = 3(x + 2)$. Any number substituted for x will result in a true statement (both sides of the equation are equal).

By manipulating equations like the two above, the variable of the equation will cancel out completely. If the remaining constants express a true statement (ex. $6 = 6$), then all real numbers are solutions to the equation. If the constants left express a false statement (ex. $3 = -1$), then no solution exists for the equation.

Solving a linear inequality requires all values that make the statement true to be determined. For example, solving $3x - 7 \geq -13$ produces the solution $x \geq -2$. This means that -2 and any number greater than -2 produces a true statement. Solution sets for linear inequalities will often be displayed using a number line. If a value is included in the set ($\geq$ or $\leq$), a shaded dot is placed on that value and an arrow extending in the direction of the solutions. For a variable > or $\geq$ a number, the arrow will point right on a number line, the direction where the numbers increase. If a variable is < or $\leq$ a number, the arrow will point left on a number line, which is the direction where the numbers decrease. If the value is not included in the set (> or <), an open (unshaded) circle on that value is used with an arrow in the appropriate direction.

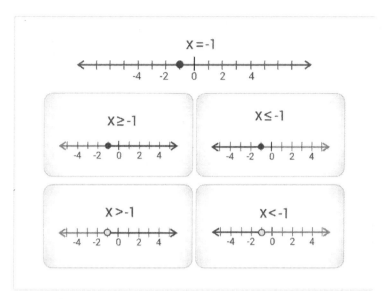

Similar to linear equations, a linear inequality may have a solution set consisting of all real numbers, or can contain no solution. When solved algebraically, a linear inequality in which the variable cancels out and results in a true statement (ex. $7 \geq 2$) has a solution set of all real numbers. A linear inequality in which the variable cancels out and results in a false statement (ex. $7 \leq 2$) has no solution.

Linear Relationships

Linear relationships describe the way two quantities change with respect to each other. The relationship is defined as linear because a line is produced if all the sets of corresponding values are graphed on a coordinate grid. When expressing the linear relationship as an equation, the equation is often written in the form $y = mx + b$ (slope-intercept form) where m and b are numerical values and x and y are variables (for example, $y = 5x + 10$). Given a linear equation and the value of either variable (x or y), the value of the other variable can be determined.

Suppose a teacher is grading a test containing 20 questions with 5 points given for each correct answer, adding a curve of 10 points to each test. This linear relationship can be expressed as the equation $y = 5x + 10$ where x represents the number of correct answers and y represents the test score. To determine the score of a test with a given number of correct answers, the number of correct answers is substituted into the equation for x and evaluated. For example, for 10 correct answers, 10 is substituted for x: $y = 5(10) + 10 \rightarrow y = 60$. Therefore, 10 correct answers will result in a score of 60. The number of correct answers needed to obtain a certain score can also be determined. To determine the number of correct answers needed to score a 90, 90 is substituted for y in the equation (y represents the test score) and solved: $90 = 5x + 10 \rightarrow 80 = 5x \rightarrow 16 = x$. Therefore, 16 correct answers are needed to score a 90.

Linear relationships may be represented by a table of 2 corresponding values. Certain tables may determine the relationship between the values and predict other corresponding sets. Consider the table below, which displays the money in a checking account that charges a monthly fee:

Month	0	1	2	3	4
Balance	$210	$195	$180	$165	$150

An examination of the values reveals that the account loses $15 every month (the month increases by one and the balance decreases by 15). This information can be used to predict future values. To determine what the value will be in month 6, the pattern can be continued, and it can be concluded that the balance will be $120. To determine which month the balance will be $0, $210 is divided by $15 (since the balance decreases $15 every month), resulting in month 14.

Similar to a table, a graph can display corresponding values of a linear relationship.

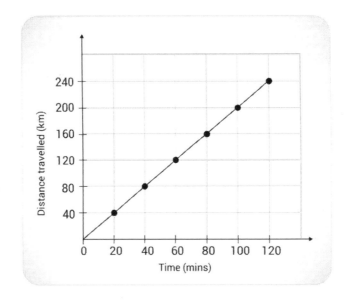

The graph above represents the relationship between distance traveled and time. To find the distance traveled in 80 minutes, the mark for 80 minutes is located at the bottom of the graph. By following this mark directly up on the graph, the corresponding point for 80 minutes is directly across from the 160 kilometer mark. This information indicates that the distance travelled in 80 minutes is 160 kilometers. To predict information not displayed on the graph, the way in which the variables change with respect to one another is determined. In this case, distance increases by 40 kilometers as time increases by 20 minutes. This information can be used to continue the data in the graph or convert the values to a table.

Number and Shape Patterns

Patterns within a sequence can come in 2 distinct forms: the items (shapes, numbers, etc.) either repeat in a constant order, or the items change from one step to another in some consistent way. The core is the smallest unit, or number of items, that repeats in a repeating pattern. For example, the pattern oo▲oo▲o… has a core that is oo▲. Knowing only the core, the pattern can be extended. Knowing the number of steps in the core allows the identification of an item in each step without drawing/writing the entire pattern out. For example, suppose the tenth item in the previous pattern must be determined. Because the core consists of three items (oo▲), the core repeats in multiples of 3. In other words, steps

3, 6, 9, 12, etc. will be ▲ completing the core with the core starting over on the next step. For the above example, the 9th step will be ▲ and the 10th will be ○.

The most common patterns in which each item changes from one step to the next are arithmetic and geometric sequences. An arithmetic sequence is one in which the items increase or decrease by a constant difference. In other words, the same thing is added or subtracted to each item or step to produce the next. To determine if a sequence is arithmetic, determine what must be added or subtracted to step one to produce step two. Then, check if the same thing is added/subtracted to step two to produce step three. The same thing must be added/subtracted to step three to produce step four, and so on. Consider the pattern 13, 10, 7, 4 . . . To get from step one (13) to step two (10) by adding or subtracting requires subtracting by 3. The next step is checking if subtracting 3 from step two (10) will produce step three (7), and subtracting 3 from step three (7) will produce step four (4). In this case, the pattern holds true. Therefore, this is an arithmetic sequence in which each step is produced by subtracting 3 from the previous step. To extend the sequence, 3 is subtracted from the last step to produce the next. The next three numbers in the sequence are 1, -2, -5.

A geometric sequence is one in which each step is produced by multiplying or dividing the previous step by the same number. To determine if a sequence is geometric, decide what step one must be multiplied or divided by to produce step two. Then check if multiplying or dividing step two by the same number produces step three, and so on. Consider the pattern 2, 8, 32, 128 . . . To get from step one (2) to step two (8) requires multiplication by 4. The next step determines if multiplying step two (8) by 4 produces step three (32), and multiplying step three (32) by 4 produces step four (128). In this case, the pattern holds true. Therefore, this is a geometric sequence in which each step is produced by multiplying the previous step by 4. To extend the sequence, the last step is multiplied by 4 and repeated. The next three numbers in the sequence are 512; 2,048; 8,192.

Although arithmetic and geometric sequences typically use numbers, these sequences can also be represented by shapes. For example, an arithmetic sequence could consist of shapes with three sides, four sides, and five sides (add one side to the previous step to produce the next). A geometric sequence could consist of eight blocks, four blocks, and two blocks (each step is produced by dividing the number of blocks in the previous step by 2).

Conjectures, Predictions, or Generalizations Based on Patterns

An arithmetic or geometric sequence can be written as a formula and used to determine unknown steps without writing out the entire sequence. (Note that a similar process for repeating patterns is covered in the previous section.) An arithmetic sequence progresses by a *common difference*. To determine the common difference, any step is subtracted by the step that precedes it. In the sequence 4, 9, 14, 19 . . . the common difference, or d, is 5. By expressing each step as a_1, a_2, a_3, etc., a formula can be written to represent the sequence. a_1 is the first step. To produce step two, step 1 (a_1) is added to the common difference (d): $a_2 = a_1 + d$. To produce step three, the common difference (d) is added twice to a_1: $a_3 = a_1 + 2d$. To produce step four, the common difference (d) is added three times to a_1: $a_4 = a_1 + 3d$. Following this pattern allows a general rule for arithmetic sequences to be written. For any term of the sequence (a_n), the first step (a_1) is added to the product of the common difference (d) and one less than the step of the term ($n - 1$): $a_n = a_1 + (n - 1)d$. Suppose the 8th term (a_8) is to be found in the previous sequence. By knowing the first step (a_1) is 4 and the common difference (d) is 5, the formula can be used: $a_n = a_1 + (n - 1)d \rightarrow a_8 = 4 + (7)5 \rightarrow a_8 = 39$.

In a geometric sequence, each step is produced by multiplying or dividing the previous step by the same number. The *common ratio*, or (r), can be determined by dividing any step by the previous step. In the sequence 1, 3, 9, 27 . . . the common ratio (r) is 3 ($\frac{3}{1} = 3$ or $\frac{9}{3} = 3$ or $\frac{27}{9} = 3$). Each successive step can be expressed as a product of the first step (a_1) and the common ratio (r) to some power. For example, $a_2 = a_1 \times r$; $a_3 = a_1 \times r \times r$ or $a_3 = a_1 \times r^2$; $a_4 = a_1 \times r \times r \times r$ or $a_4 = a\_1 \times r^3$. Following this pattern, a general rule for geometric sequences can be written. For any term of the sequence (a_n), the first step (a_1) is multiplied by the common ratio (r) raised to the power one less than the step of the term ($n - 1$): $a_n = a_1 \times r^{(n-1)}$. Suppose for the previous sequence, the 7th term (a_7) is to be found. Knowing the first step (a_1) is one, and the common ratio (r) is 3, the formula can be used: $a_n = a_1 \times r^{(n-1)} \rightarrow a_7 = (1) \times 3^6 \rightarrow a_7 = 729$.

Corresponding Terms of Two Numerical Patterns

When given two numerical patterns, the corresponding terms should be examined to determine if a relationship exists between them. Corresponding terms between patterns are the pairs of numbers that appear in the same step of the two sequences. Consider the following patterns 1, 2, 3, 4 . . . and 3, 6, 9, 12 . . . The corresponding terms are: 1 and 3; 2 and 6; 3 and 9; and 4 and 12. To identify the relationship, each pair of corresponding terms is examined and the possibilities of performing an operation (+, −, ×, ÷) to the term from the first sequence to produce the corresponding term in the second sequence are determined. In this case:

$1 + 2 = 3$	or	$1 \times 3 = 3$
$2 + 4 = 6$	or	$2 \times 3 = 6$
$3 + 6 = 9$	or	$3 \times 3 = 9$
$4 + 8 = 12$	or	$4 \times 3 = 12$

The consistent pattern is that the number from the first sequence multiplied by 3 equals its corresponding term in the second sequence. By assigning each sequence a label (input and output) or variable (x and y), the relationship can be written as an equation. If the first sequence represents the inputs, or x, and the second sequence represents the outputs, or y, the relationship can be expressed as: $y = 3x$.

Consider the following sets of numbers:

a	2	4	6	8
b	6	8	10	12

To write a rule for the relationship between the values for a and the values for b, the corresponding terms (2 and 6; 4 and 8; 6 and 10; 8 and 12) are examined. The possibilities for producing b from a are:

$2 + 4 = 6$	or	$2 \times 3 = 6$
$4 + 4 = 8$	or	$4 \times 2 = 8$
$6 + 4 = 10$		
$8 + 4 = 12$	or	$8 \times 1.5 = 12$

The consistent pattern is that adding 4 to the value of *a* produces the value of *b*. The relationship can be written as the equation $a + 4 = b$.

Geometry

Geometry is part of mathematics. It deals with shapes and their properties. Geometry means knowing the names and properties of shapes. It is also similar to measurement and number operations. The basis of geometry involves being able to label and describe shapes and their properties. That knowledge will lead to working with formulas such as area, perimeter, and volume. This knowledge will help to solve word problems involving shapes.

Flat or two-dimensional shapes include circles, triangles, hexagons, and rectangles, among others. Three-dimensional solid shapes, such as spheres and cubes, are also used in geometry. A shape can be classified based on whether it is open like the letter U or closed like the letter O. Further classifications involve counting the number of sides and vertices (corners) on the shapes. This will help you tell the difference between shapes.

Polygons can be drawn by sketching a fixed number of line segments that meet to create a closed shape. In addition, *triangles* can be drawn by sketching a closed space using only three line segments. *Quadrilaterals* are closed shapes with four line segments. Note that a triangle has three vertices, and a quadrilateral has four vertices.

To draw circles, one curved line segment must be drawn that has only one endpoint. This creates a closed shape. Given such direction, every point on the line would be the same distance away from its center. The radius of a circle goes from an endpoint on the center of the circle to an endpoint on the circle. The diameter is the line segment created by placing an endpoint on the circle, drawing through the radius, and placing the other endpoint on the circle. A compass can be used to draw circles of a more precise size and shape.

Area and Perimeter
Area relates to two-dimensional geometric shapes. Basically, a figure is divided into two-dimensional units. The number of units needed to cover the figure is counted. Area is measured using square units, such as square inches, feet, centimeters, or kilometers.

Perimeter is the length of all its sides. The perimeter of a given closed sided figure would be found by first measuring the length of each side and then calculating the sum of all sides.

Formulas can be used to calculate area and perimeter. The area of a rectangle is found by multiplying its length, *l,* times its width, *w.* Therefore, the formula for area is $A = l \times w$. An equivalent expression is found by using the term base, *b,* instead of length, to represent the horizontal side of the shape. In this case, the formula is $A = b \times h$. This same formula can be used for all parallelograms. Here is a visualization of a rectangle with its labeled sides:

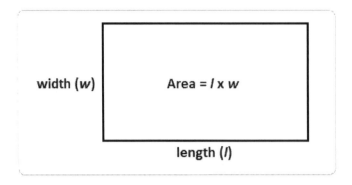

A square has four equal sides with the length s. Its length is equal to its width. The formula for the area of a square is $A = s \times s$. Finally, the area of a triangle is calculated by dividing the area of the rectangle that would be formed by the base, the altitude, and height of the triangle. Therefore, the area of a triangle is $A = \frac{1}{2} \times b \times h$. Formulas for perimeter are derived by adding length measurements of the sides of a figure. The perimeter of a rectangle is the result of adding the length of the four sides. Therefore, the formula for perimeter of a rectangle is $P = 2 \times l + 2 \times w$, and the formula for perimeter of a square is $P = 4 \times s$. The perimeter of a triangle would be the sum of the lengths of the three sides.

Volume

Volume is a measurement of the amount of space that in a 3-dimensional figure. Volume is measured using cubic units, such as cubic inches, feet, centimeters, or kilometers.

Say you have 10 playing die that are each one cubic centimeter. Say you placed these along the length of a rectangle. Then 8 die are placed along its width. The remaining area is filled in with die. There would be 80 die in total. This would equal a volume of 80 cubic centimeters. Say the shape is doubled so that its height consists of two cube lengths. There would be 160 cubes. Also, its volume would be 160 cubic centimeters. Adding another level of cubes would mean that there would be $3 \times 80 = 240$ cubes. This idea shows that volume is calculated by multiplying area times height. The actual formula for volume of a three-dimensional rectangular solid is $V = l \times w \times h$. In this formula *l* represents length, *w* represents width, and *h* represents height. Volume can also be thought of as area of the base times the height. The base in this case would be the entire rectangle formed by *l* and *w*. Here is an example of a rectangular solid with labeled sides:

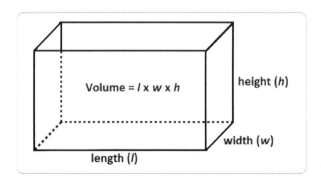

A *cube* is a special type of rectangular solid in which its length, width, and height are the same. If this length is s, then the formula for the volume of a cube is $V = s \times s \times s$.

Lines and Angles

In geometry, a *line* connects two points, has no thickness, and extends indefinitely in both directions beyond the points. If it does end at two points, it is known as a *line segment*. It is important to distinguish between a line and a line segment.

An angle can be visualized as a corner. It is defined as the formation of two rays connecting at a vertex that extend indefinitely. Angles are measured in degrees. Their measurement is a measure of rotation. A full rotation equals 360 degrees and represents a circle. Half of a rotation equals 180 degrees and represents a half-circle. Subsequently, 90 degrees represents a quarter-circle. Similar to the hands on a clock, an angle begins at the center point, and two lines extend indefinitely from that point in two different directions.

A clock can be useful when learning how to measure angles. At 3:00, the big hand is on the 12 and the small hand is on the 3. The angle formed is 90 degrees and is known as a *right angle*. Any angle less than 90 degrees, such as the one formed at 2:00, is known as an *acute angle*. Any angle greater than 90 degrees is known as an *obtuse angle*. The entire clock represents 360 degrees, and each clockwise increment on the clock represents an addition of 30 degrees. Therefore, 6:00 represents 180 degrees, 7:00 represents 210 degrees, etc. Angle measurement is additive. An angle can be broken into two non-overlapping angles. The total measure of the larger angle is equal to the sum of the measurements of the two smaller angles.

A *ray* is a straight path that has an endpoint on one end and extends indefinitely in the other direction. Lines are known as being *coplanar* if they are located in the same plane. Coplanar lines exist within the same two-dimensional surface. Two lines are *parallel* if they are coplanar, extend in the same direction, and never cross. They are known as being *equidistant* because they are always the same distance from each other. If lines do cross, they are known as *intersecting lines*. As discussed previously, angles are utilized throughout geometry, and their measurement can be seen through the use of an analog clock. An angle is formed when two rays begin at the same endpoint. *Adjacent angles* can be formed by forming two angles out of one shared ray. They are two side-by-side angles that also share an endpoint.

Perpendicular lines are coplanar lines that form a right angle at their point of intersection. A triangle that contains a right angle is known as a *right triangle*. The sum of the angles within any triangle is always 180 degrees. Therefore, in a right triangle, the sum of the two angles that are not right angles is 90 degrees. Any two angles that sum up to 90 degrees are known as *complementary angles*. A triangle that contains an obtuse angle is known as an *obtuse triangle*. A triangle that contains three acute angles is known as an *acute triangle*. Here is an example of a 180-degree angle, split up into an acute and obtuse angle:

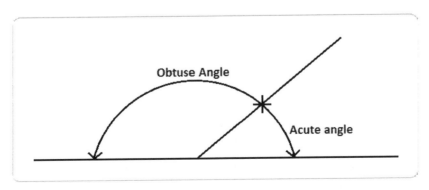

The vocabulary regarding many two-dimensional shapes is important to understand and use appropriately. Many four-sided figures can be identified using properties of angles and lines. A *quadrilateral* is a closed shape with four sides. A *parallelogram* is a specific type of quadrilateral that has two sets of parallel lines having the same length. A *trapezoid* is a quadrilateral having only one set of parallel sides. A *rectangle* is a parallelogram that has four right angles. A *rhombus* is a parallelogram with two acute angles, two obtuse angles, and four equal sides. The acute angles are of equal measure, and the obtuse angles are of equal measure. Finally, a *square* is a rhombus consisting of four right angles. It is important to note that some of these shapes share common attributes. For instance, all four-sided shapes are quadrilaterals. All squares are rectangles, but not all rectangles are squares.

Symmetry is another concept in geometry. If a two-dimensional shape can be folded along a straight line and the halves line up exactly, the figure is *symmetric*. The line is known as a *line of symmetry*. Circles, squares, and rectangles are examples of symmetric shapes.

Measurement

Measuring Lengths of Objects

The length of an object can be measured using standard tools such as rulers, yard sticks, meter sticks, and measuring tapes. The following image depicts a yardstick:

Choosing the right tool to perform the measurement requires determining whether United States customary units or metric units are desired, and having a grasp of the approximate length of each unit and the approximate length of each tool. The measurement can still be performed by trial and error without the knowledge of the approximate size of the tool.

For example, to determine the length of a room in feet, a United States customary unit, various tools can be used for this task. These include a ruler (typically 12 inches/1 foot long), a yardstick (3 feet/1 yard long), or a tape measure displaying feet (typically either 25 feet or 50 feet). Because the length of a room is much larger than the length of a ruler or a yardstick, a tape measure should be used to perform the measurement.

When the correct measuring tool is selected, the measurement is performed by first placing the tool directly above or below the object (if making a horizontal measurement) or directly next to the object (if making a vertical measurement). The next step is aligning the tool so that one end of the object is at the mark for zero units, then recording the unit of the mark at the other end of the object. To give the length of a paperclip in metric units, a ruler displaying centimeters is aligned with one end of the paper clip to the mark for zero centimeters.

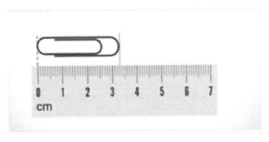

Directly down from the other end of the paperclip is the mark that measures its length. In this case, that mark is two small dashes past the 3 centimeter mark. Each small dash is 1 millimeter (or .1 centimeters). Therefore, the length of the paper clip is 3.2 centimeters.

To compare the lengths of objects, each length must be expressed in the same unit. If possible, the objects should be measured with the same tool or with tools utilizing the same units. For example, a ruler and a yardstick can both measure length in inches. If the lengths of the objects are expressed in different units, these different units must be converted to the same unit before comparing them. If two lengths are expressed in the same unit, the lengths may be compared by subtracting the smaller value from the larger value. For example, suppose the lengths of two gardens are to be compared. Garden A has a length of 4 feet, and garden B has a length of 2 yards. 2 yards is converted to 6 feet so that the measurements have similar units. Then, the smaller length (4 feet) is subtracted from the larger length (6ft): 6ft – 4ft = 2ft. Therefore, garden B is 2 feet larger than garden A.

Relative Sizes of United States Customary Units and Metric Units

The United States customary system and the metric system each consist of distinct units to measure lengths and volume of liquids. The U.S. customary units for length, from smallest to largest, are: inch (in), foot (ft), yard (yd), and mile (mi). The metric units for length, from smallest to largest, are: millimeter (mm), centimeter (cm), decimeter (dm), meter (m), and kilometer (km). The relative size of each unit of length is shown below.

U.S. Customary	Metric	Conversion
12in = 1ft	10mm = 1cm	1in = 254cm
36in = 3ft = 1yd	10cm = 1dm(decimeter)	1m ≈ 3.28ft ≈ 1.09yd
5,280ft = 1,760yd = 1mi	100cm = 10dm = 1m	1mi ≈ 1.6km
	1000m = 1km	

The U.S. customary units for volume of liquids, from smallest to largest, are: fluid ounces (fl oz), cup (c), pint (pt), quart (qt), and gallon (gal). The metric units for volume of liquids, from smallest to largest, are: milliliter (mL), centiliter (cL), deciliter (dL), liter (L), and kiloliter (kL). The relative size of each unit of liquid volume is shown below.

U.S. Customary	Metric	Conversion
8fl oz = 1c	10mL = 1cL	1pt ≈ 0.473L
2c = 1pt	10cL = 1dL	1L ≈ 1.057qt
4c = 2pt = 1qt	1,000mL = 100cL = 10dL = 1L	1gal ≈ 3,785L
4qt = 1gal	1,000L = 1kL	

The U.S. customary system measures weight (how strongly Earth is pulling on an object) in the following units, from least to greatest: ounce (oz), pound (lb), and ton. The metric system measures mass (the quantity of matter within an object) in the following units, from least to greatest: milligram (mg), centigram (cg), gram (g), kilogram (kg), and metric ton (MT). The relative sizes of each unit of weight and mass are shown below.

U.S. Measures of Weight	Metric Measures of Mass
16oz = 1lb	10mg = 1cg
2,000lb = 1 ton	100cg = 1g
	1,000g = 1kg
	1,000kg = 1MT

Note that weight and mass DO NOT measure the same thing.

Time is measured in the following units, from shortest to longest: second (sec), minute (min), hour (h), day (d), week (wk), month (mo), year (yr), decade, century, millennium. The relative sizes of each unit of time is shown below.

- 60sec = 1min
- 60min = 1h
- 24hr = 1d
- 7d = 1wk
- 52wk = 1yr
- 12mo = 1yr
- 10yr = 1 decade
- 100yrs = 1 century
- 1,000yrs = 1 millennium

Conversion of Units

When working with different systems of measurement, conversion from one unit to another may be necessary. The conversion rate must be known to convert units. One method for converting units is to write and solve a proportion. The arrangement of values in a proportion is extremely important. Suppose that a problem requires converting 20 fluid ounces to cups. To do so, a proportion can be written using the conversion rate of 8fl oz = 1c with x representing the missing value. The proportion can be written in any of the following ways:

$$\frac{1}{8} = \frac{x}{20} \left(\frac{c \; for \; conversion}{fl \; oz \; for \; conversion} = \frac{unknown \; c}{fl \; oz \; given} \right); \frac{8}{1} = \frac{20}{x} \left(\frac{fl \; oz \; for \; conversion}{c \; for \; conversion} = \frac{fl \; oz \; given}{unknown \; c} \right);$$

$$\frac{1}{x} = \frac{8}{20} \left(\frac{c \; for \; conversion}{unknown \; c} = \frac{fl \; oz \; for \; conversion}{fl \; oz \; given} \right); \frac{x}{1} = \frac{20}{8} \left(\frac{unknown \; c}{c \; for \; conversion} = \frac{fl \; oz \; given}{fl \; oz \; for \; conversion} \right)$$

To solve a proportion, the ratios are cross-multiplied and the resulting equation is solved. When cross-multiplying, all four proportions above will produce the same equation: $(8)(x) = (20)(1) \rightarrow 8x = 20$. Dividing by 8 to isolate the variable x, the result is $x = 2.5$. The variable x represented the unknown number of cups. Therefore, the conclusion is that 20 fluid ounces converts (is equal) to 2.5 cups.

Sometimes converting units requires writing and solving more than one proportion. Suppose an exam question asks to determine how many hours are in 2 weeks. Without knowing the conversion rate between hours and weeks, this can be determined knowing the conversion rates between weeks and days, and between days and hours. First, weeks are converted to days, then days are converted to hours. To convert from weeks to days, the following proportion can be written:

$$\frac{7}{1} = \frac{x}{2} \left(\frac{days\ conversion}{weeks\ conversion} = \frac{days\ unknown}{weeks\ given} \right)$$

Cross-multiplying produces: $(7)(2) = (x)(1) \rightarrow 14 = x$. Therefore, 2 weeks is equal to 14 days. Next, a proportion is written to convert 14 days to hours: $\frac{24}{1} = \frac{x}{14} \left(\frac{conversion\ hours}{conversion\ days} = \frac{unknown\ hours}{given\ days} \right)$. Cross-multiplying produces: $(24)(14) = (x)(1) \rightarrow 336 = x$. Therefore, the answer is that there are 336 hours in 2 weeks.

Data Analysis and Probability

Measures of Center and Range

The center of a set of data (statistical values) can be represented by its mean, median, or mode. These are sometimes referred to as measures of central tendency. The mean is the average of the data set. The mean can be calculated by adding the data values and dividing by the sample size (the number of data points). Suppose a student has test scores of 93, 84, 88, 72, 91, and 77. To find the mean, or average, the scores are added and the sum is divided by 6 because there are 6 test scores: $\frac{93+84+88+72+91+77}{6} = \frac{505}{6} = 84.17$.

Given the mean of a data set and the sum of the data points, the sample size can be determined by dividing the sum by the mean. Suppose you are told that Kate averaged 12 points per game and scored a total of 156 points for the season. The number of games that she played (the sample size or the number of data points) can be determined by dividing the total points (sum of data points) by her average (mean of data points): $\frac{156}{12} = 13$. Therefore, Kate played in 13 games this season.

If given the mean of a data set and the sample size, the sum of the data points can be determined by multiplying the mean and sample size. Suppose you are told that Tom worked 6 days last week for an average of 5.5 hours per day. The total number of hours worked for the week (sum of data points) can be determined by multiplying his daily average (mean of data points) by the number of days worked (sample size): $5.5 \times 6 = 33$. Therefore, Tom worked a total of 33 hours last week.

The median of a data set is the value of the data point in the middle when the sample is arranged in numerical order. To find the median of a data set, the values are written in order from least to greatest. The lowest and highest values are simultaneously eliminated, repeating until the value in the middle remains. Suppose the salaries of math teachers are: \$35,000; \$38,500; \$41,000; \$42,000; \$42,000; \$44,500; \$49,000. The values are listed from least to greatest to find the median. The lowest and highest values are eliminated until only the middle value remains. Repeating this step three times reveals a median salary of $42,000. If the sample set has an even number of data points, two values will remain after all others are eliminated. In this case, the mean of the two middle values is the median. Consider the following data set: 7, 9, 10, 13, 14, 14. Eliminating the lowest and highest values twice leaves two values, 10 and 13, in the middle. The mean of these values $\left(\frac{10+13}{2}\right)$ is the median. Therefore, the set has a median of 11.5.

The mode of a data set is the value that appears most often. A data set may have a single mode, multiple modes, or no mode. If different values repeat equally as often, multiple modes exist. If no value repeats, no mode exists. Consider the following data sets:

- A: 7, 9, 10, 13, 14, 14
- B: 37, 44, 33, 37, 49, 44, 51, 34, 37, 33, 44
- C: 173, 154, 151, 168, 155

Set A has a mode of 14. Set B has modes of 37 and 44. Set C has no mode.

The range of a data set is the difference between the highest and the lowest values in the set. The range can be considered the span of the data set. To determine the range, the smallest value in the set is subtracted from the largest value. The ranges for the data sets A, B, and C above are calculated as follows: A: $14 - 7 = 7$; B: $51 - 33 = 18$; C: $173 - 151 = 22$.

Best Description of a Set of Data
Measures of central tendency, namely mean, median, and mode, describe characteristics of a set of data. Specifically, they are intended to represent a *typical* value in the set by identifying a central position of the set. Depending on the characteristics of a specific set of data, different measures of central tendency are more indicative of a typical value in the set.

When a data set is grouped closely together with a relatively small range and the data is spread out somewhat evenly, the mean is an effective indicator of a typical value in the set. Consider the following data set representing the height of sixth grade boys in inches: 61 inches, 54 inches, 58 inches, 63 inches, 58 inches. The mean of the set is 58.8 inches. The data set is grouped closely (the range is only 9 inches) and the values are spread relatively evenly (three values below the mean and two values above the mean). Therefore, the mean value of 58.8 inches is an effective measure of central tendency in this case.

When a data set contains a small number of values either extremely large or extremely small when compared to the other values, the mean is not an effective measure of central tendency. Consider the following data set representing annual incomes of homeowners on a given street: $71,000; $74,000; $75,000; $77,000; $340,000. The mean of this set is $127,400. This figure does not indicate a typical value in the set, which contains four out of five values between $71,000 and $77,000. The median is a much more effective measure of central tendency for data sets such as these. Finding the middle value diminishes the influence of outliers, or numbers that may appear out of place, like the $340,000 annual income. The median for this set is $75,000 which is much more typical of a value in the set.

The mode of a data set is a useful measure of central tendency for categorical data when each piece of data is an option from a category. Consider a survey of 31 commuters asking how they get to work with results summarized below.

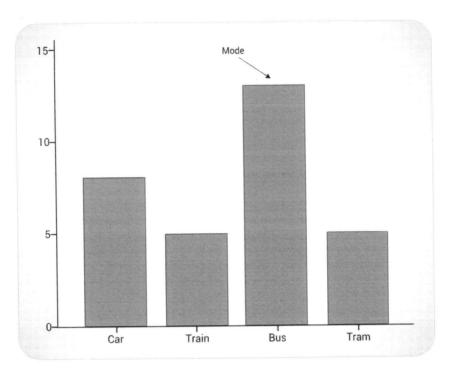

The mode for this set represents the value, or option, of the data that repeats most often. This indicates that the bus is the most popular method of transportation for the commuters.

<u>Effects of Changes in Data</u>
Changing all values of a data set in a consistent way produces predictable changes in the measures of the center and range of the set. A linear transformation changes the original value into the new value by either adding a given number to each value, multiplying each value by a given number, or both. Adding (or subtracting) a given value to each data point will increase (or decrease) the mean, median, and any modes by the same value. However, the range will remain the same due to the way that range is calculated. Multiplying (or dividing) a given value by each data point will increase (or decrease) the mean, median, and any modes, and the range by the same factor.

Consider the following data set, call it set P, representing the price of different cases of soda at a grocery store: $4.25, $4.40, $4.75, $4.95, $4.95, $5.15. The mean of set P is $4.74. The median is $4.85. The mode of the set is $4.95. The range is $0.90. Suppose the state passes a new tax of $0.25 on every case of soda sold. The new data set, set T, is calculated by adding $0.25 to each data point from set P. Therefore, set T consists of the following values: $4.50, $4.65, $5.00, $5.20, $5.20, $5.40. The mean of set T is $4.99. The median is $5.10. The mode of the set is $5.20. The range is $.90. The mean, median and mode of set T is equal to $0.25 added to the mean, median, and mode of set P. The range stays the same.

Now suppose, due to inflation, the store raises the cost of every item by 10 percent. Raising costs by 10 percent is calculated by multiplying each value by 1.1. The new data set, set I, is calculated by multiplying each data point from set T by 1.1. Therefore, set I consists of the following values: $4.95,

$5.12, $5.50, $5.72, $5.72, $5.94. The mean of set *I* is $5.49. The median is $5.61. The mode of the set is $5.72. The range is $0.99. The mean, median, mode, and range of set *I* is equal to 1.1 multiplied by the mean, median, mode, and range of set *T* because each increased by a factor of 10 percent.

Describing a Set of Data

A set of data can be described in terms of its center, spread, shape and any unusual features. The center of a data set can be measured by its mean, median, or mode. Measures of central tendency are covered in the *Measures of Center and Range* section. The spread of a data set refers to how far the data points are from the center (mean or median). The spread can be measured by the range or the quartiles and interquartile range. A data set with data points clustered around the center will have a small spread. A data set covering a wide range will have a large spread.

When a data set is displayed as a histogram or frequency distribution plot, the shape indicates if a sample is normally distributed, symmetrical, or has measures of skewness or kurtosis. When graphed, a data set with a normal distribution will resemble a bell curve.

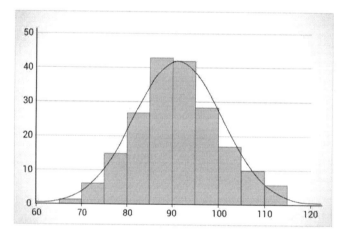

If the data set is symmetrical, each half of the graph when divided at the center is a mirror image of the other. If the graph has fewer data points to the right, the data is skewed right. If it has fewer data points to the left, the data is skewed left.

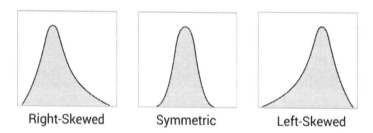

Right-Skewed   Symmetric   Left-Skewed

Kurtosis is a measure of whether the data is heavy-tailed with a high number of outliers, or light-tailed with a low number of outliers.

A description of a data set should include any unusual features such as gaps or outliers. A gap is a span within the range of the data set containing no data points. An outlier is a data point with a value either extremely large or extremely small when compared to the other values in the set.

Interpreting Displays of Data

A set of data can be visually displayed in various forms allowing for quick identification of characteristics of the set. Histograms, such as the one shown below, display the number of data points (vertical axis) that fall into given intervals (horizontal axis) across the range of the set. The histogram below displays the heights of black cherry trees in a certain city park. Each rectangle represents the number of trees with heights between a given five-point span. For example, the furthest bar to the right indicates that two trees are between 85 and 90 feet. Histograms can describe the center, spread, shape, and any unusual characteristics of a data set.

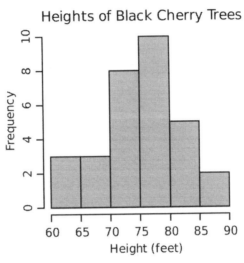

A box plot, also called a box-and-whisker plot, divides the data points into four groups and displays the five number summary for the set, as well as any outliers. The five number summary consists of:

- The lower extreme: the lowest value that is not an outlier
- The higher extreme: the highest value that is not an outlier
- The median of the set: also referred to as the second quartile or Q_2
- The first quartile or Q_1: the median of values below Q_2
- The third quartile or Q_3: the median of values above Q_2

Calculating each of these values is covered in the next section, *Graphical Representation of Data*.

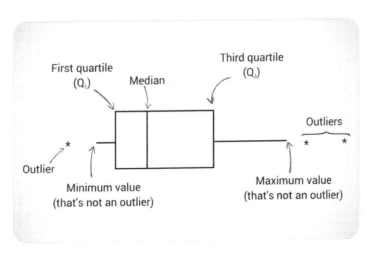

Suppose the box plot displays IQ scores for 12th grade students at a given school. The five number summary of the data consists of: lower extreme (67); upper extreme (127); Q_2 or median (100); Q_1 (91); Q_3 (108); and outliers (135 and 140). Although all data points are not known from the plot, the points are divided into four quartiles each, including 25% of the data points. Therefore, 25% of students scored between 67 and 91, 25% scored between 91 and 100, 25% scored between 100 and 108, and 25% scored between 108 and 127. These percentages include the normal values for the set and exclude the outliers. This information is useful when comparing a given score with the rest of the scores in the set.

A scatter plot is a mathematical diagram that visually displays the relationship or connection between two variables. The independent variable is placed on the x-axis, or horizontal axis, and the dependent variable is placed on the y-axis, or vertical axis. When visually examining the points on the graph, if the points model a linear relationship, or a line of best-fit can be drawn through the points with the points relatively close on either side, then a correlation exists. If the line of best-fit has a positive slope (rises from left to right), then the variables have a positive correlation. If the line of best-fit has a negative slope (falls from left to right), then the variables have a negative correlation. If a line of best-fit cannot be drawn, then no correlation exists. A positive or negative correlation can be categorized as strong or weak, depending on how closely the points are graphed around the line of best-fit.

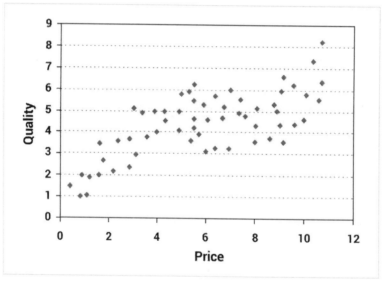

Graphical Representation of Data

Various graphs can be used to visually represent a given set of data. Each type of graph requires a different method of arranging data points and different calculations of the data. Examples of histograms, box plots, and scatter plots are discussed in the previous section *Interpreting Displays of Data*. To construct a histogram, the range of the data points is divided into equal intervals. The frequency for each interval is then determined, which reveals how many points fall into each interval. A graph is constructed with the vertical axis representing the frequency and the horizontal axis representing the intervals. The lower value of each interval should be labeled along the horizontal axis. Finally, for each interval, a bar is drawn from the lower value of each interval to the lower value of the next interval with a height equal to the frequency of the interval. Because of the intervals, histograms do not have any gaps between bars along the horizontal axis.

A scatter plot displays the relationship between two variables. Values for the independent variable, typically denoted by *x*, are paired with values for the dependent variable, typically denoted by *y*. Each set of corresponding values are written as an ordered pair (*x*, *y*). To construct the graph, a coordinate grid is labeled with the *x*-axis representing the independent variable and the *y*-axis representing the dependent variable. Each ordered pair is graphed.

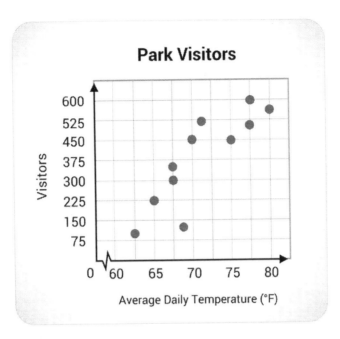

Like a scatter plot, a line graph compares variables that change continuously, typically over time. Paired data values (ordered pair) are plotted on a coordinate grid with the *x*- and *y*-axis representing the variables. A line is drawn from each point to the next, going from left to right. The line graph below displays cell phone use for given years (two variables) for men, women, and both sexes (three data sets).

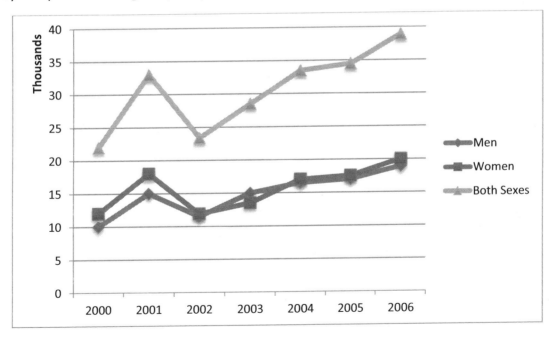

A line plot, also called dot plot, displays the frequency of data (numerical values) on a number line. To construct a line plot, a number line is used that includes all unique data values. It is marked with x's or dots above the value the number of times that the value occurs in the data set.

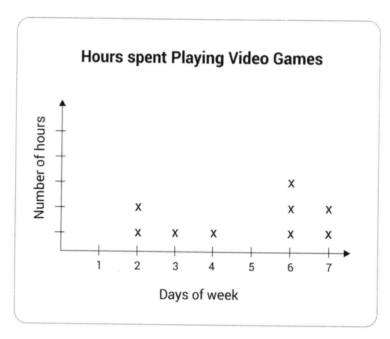

A bar graph looks similar to a histogram but displays categorical data. The horizontal axis represents each category and the vertical axis represents the frequency for the category. A bar is drawn for each category (often different colors) with a height extending to the frequency for that category within the data set. A double bar graph displays two sets of data that contain data points consisting of the same categories. The double bar graph below indicates that two girls and four boys like Pad Thai the most out of all the foods, two boys and five girls like pizza, and so on.

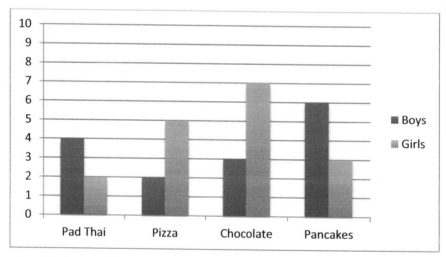

A circle graph, also called a pie chart, displays categorical data with each category representing a percentage of the whole data set. To construct a circle graph, the percent of the data set for each category must be determined. To do so, the frequency of the category is divided by the total number of data points and converted to a percent. For example, if 80 people were asked their favorite pizza topping and 20 responded cheese, then cheese constitutes 25% of the data ($\frac{20}{80} = .25 = 25\%$). Each category in a data set is represented by a *slice* of the circle proportionate to its percentage of the whole.

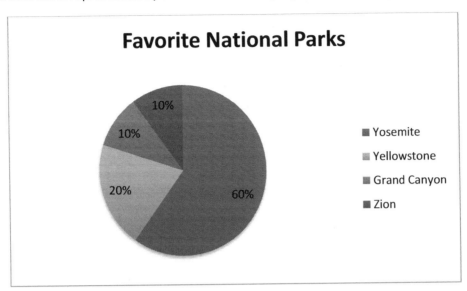

Choice of Graphs to Display Data

Choosing the appropriate graph to display a data set depends on what type of data is included in the set and what information must be displayed. Histograms and box plots can be used for data sets consisting of individual values across a wide range. Examples include test scores and incomes. Histograms and box plots will indicate the center, spread, range, and outliers of a data set. A histogram will show the shape of the data set, while a box plot will divide the set into quartiles (25% increments), allowing for comparison between a given value and the entire set.

Scatter plots and line graphs can be used to display data consisting of two variables. Examples include height and weight, or distance and time. A correlation between the variables is determined by examining the points on the graph. Line graphs are used if each value for one variable pairs with a distinct value for the other variable. Line graphs show relationships between variables.

Line plots, bar graphs, and circle graphs are all used to display categorical data, such as surveys. Line plots and bar graphs both indicate the frequency of each category within the data set. A line plot is used when the categories consist of numerical values. For example, the number of hours of TV watched by individuals is displayed on a line plot. A bar graph is used when the categories consists of words. For example, the favorite ice cream of individuals is displayed with a bar graph. A circle graph can be used to display either type of categorical data. However, unlike line plots and bar graphs, a circle graph does not indicate the frequency of each category. Instead, the circle graph represents each category as its percentage of the whole data set.

Probabilities Relative to Likelihood of Occurrence

Probability is a measure of how likely an event is to occur. Probability is written as a fraction between zero and one. If an event has a probability of zero, the event will never occur. If an event has a probability of one, the event will definitely occur. If the probability of an event is closer to zero, the event is unlikely to occur. If the probability of an event is closer to one, the event is more likely to occur. For example, a probability of $\frac{1}{2}$ means that the event is equally as likely to occur as it is not to occur. An example of this is tossing a coin. To calculate the probability of an event, the number of favorable outcomes is divided by the number of total outcomes. For example, suppose you have 2 raffle tickets out of 20 total tickets sold. The probability that you win the raffle is calculated: $\frac{number\ of\ favorable\ outcomes}{total\ number\ of\ outcomes} = \frac{2}{20} = \frac{1}{10}$ (always reduce fractions). Therefore, the probability of winning the raffle is $\frac{1}{10}$ or 0.1.

Chance is the measure of how likely an event is to occur, written as a percent. If an event will never occur, the event has a 0% chance. If an event will certainly occur, the event has a 100% chance. If an event will sometimes occur, the event has a chance somewhere between 0% and 100%. To calculate chance, probability is calculated and the fraction is converted to a percent.

The probability of multiple events occurring can be determined by multiplying the probability of each event. For example, suppose you flip a coin with heads and tails, and roll a six-sided dice numbered one through six. To find the probability that you will flip heads AND roll a two, the probability of each event is determined and those fractions are multiplied. The probability of flipping heads is $\frac{1}{2}\left(\frac{1\ side\ with\ heads}{2\ sides\ total}\right)$ and the probability of rolling a two is $\frac{1}{6}\left(\frac{1\ side\ with\ a\ 2}{6\ total\ sides}\right)$. The probability of flipping heads AND rolling a 2 is: $\frac{1}{2} \times \frac{1}{6} = \frac{1}{12}$.

The above scenario with flipping a coin and rolling a dice is an example of independent events. Independent events are circumstances in which the outcome of one event does not affect the outcome of the other event. Conversely, dependent events are ones in which the outcome of one event affects the outcome of the second event. Consider the following scenario: a bag contains 5 black marbles and 5 white marbles. What is the probability of picking 2 black marbles without replacing the marble after the first pick?

The probability of picking a black marble on the first pick is $\frac{5}{10}\left(\frac{5\ black\ marbles}{10\ total\ marbles}\right)$. Assuming that a black marble was picked, there are now 4 black marbles and 5 white marbles for the second pick. Therefore, the probability of picking a black marble on the second pick is $\frac{4}{9}\left(\frac{4\ black\ marbles}{9\ total\ marbles}\right)$. To find the probability of picking two black marbles, the probability of each is multiplied: $\frac{5}{10} \times \frac{4}{9} = \frac{20}{90} = \frac{2}{9}$.

work from left to right   ① Parenthesis   ④ Division
                             ② Exponents   ⑤ Addition
                             ③ multiplication ⑥ Subtraction

Quantitative Reasoning Practice Questions

1. In the following expression, which operation should be completed first? $5 \times 6 + 4 \div 2 - 1.$
   a. Multiplication
   b. Addition
   c. Division
   d. Subtraction

   M
   D
   A
   S

2. Which of the following is the definition of a prime number?
   a. A number that factors only into itself and one
   b. A number greater than zero that factors only into itself and one
   c. A number less than 10
   d. A number divisible by 10

   ✓

3. What of the following is the correct order of operations? p. 34
   a. Parentheses, Exponents, Multiplication, Division, Addition, Subtraction
   b. Exponents, Parentheses, Multiplication, Division, Addition, Subtraction
   c. Parentheses, Exponents, Addition, Multiplication, Division, Subtraction
   d. Parentheses, Exponents, Division, Addition, Subtraction, Multiplication

   ✓

4. If you were showing your friend how to round 245.2678 to the nearest thousandth, which place value would be used to decide whether to round up or round down? p. 27 and 29
   a. Ten-thousandth   245.2680
   b. Thousandth
   c. Hundredth
   d. Thousand

   X

5. Carey bought 184 pounds of fertilizer to use on her lawn. Each segment of her lawn required $12\frac{1}{2}$ pounds of fertilizer to do a sufficient job. If asked to determine how many segments could be fertilized with the amount purchased, what operation would be necessary to solve this problem?
   a. Multiplication
   b. Division
   c. Addition
   d. Subtraction

6. It is necessary to line up decimal places within the given numbers before performing which of the following operations?
   a. Multiplication
   b. Division
   c. Subtraction
   d. Fractions

7. Which of the following expressions best exemplifies the additive and subtractive identity?
   a. $5 + 2 - 0 = 5 + 2 + 0$
   b. $6 + x = 6 - 6$
   c. $9 - 9 = 0$
   d. $8 + 2 = 10$

8. Which four-sided shape is always a rectangle?
    a. Rhombus
    b. Square
    c. Parallelogram
    d. Quadrilateral

9. What unit of volume is used to describe the following 3-dimensional shape?

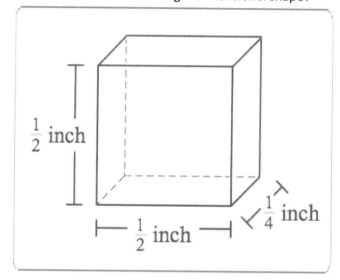

    a. Square inches
    b. Inches
    c. Cubic inches
    d. Squares

10. Which common denominator would be used in order to evaluate $\frac{2}{3} + \frac{4}{5}$?
    a. 15
    b. 3
    c. 5
    d. 10

11. In order to calculate the perimeter of a legal sized piece of paper that is 14 in and $8\frac{1}{2}$ in wide, what formula would be used?
    a. $P = 14 + 8\frac{1}{2}$

    b. $P = 14 + 8\frac{1}{2} + 14 + 8\frac{1}{2}$

    c. $P = 14 \times 8\frac{1}{2}$

    d. $P = 14 \times \frac{17}{2}$

12. Which of the following are units in the metric system?
    a. Inches, feet, miles, pounds
    b. Millimeters, centimeters, meters, pounds
    c. Kilograms, grams, kilometers, meters
    d. Teaspoons, tablespoons, ounces

13. Which important mathematical property is shown in the following expression?
$(7 \times 3) \times 2 = 7 \times (3 \times 2)$?
    a. Distributive property
    b. Commutative property
    c. Associative property
    d. Multiplicative inverse

14. The diameter of a circle measures 5.75 centimeters. What tool could be used to draw such a circle?
    a. Ruler
    b. Meter stick
    c. Compass
    d. Yard stick

15. Which of the following would be an instance in which ordinal numbers are used?
    a. Katie scored a 9 out of 10 on her quiz.
    b. Matthew finished second in the spelling bee.
    c. Jacob missed one day of school last month.
    d. Kim was 5 minutes late to school this morning.

16. Which of the following is represented by $6,000 + 400 + 30 + 6 + .5 + .08$?
    a. 6,436.58
    b. 6,346.58
    c. 64,365.8
    d. 6,436.058

17. What method is used to convert a fraction to a decimal?
    a. Divide the denominator by the numerator.
    b. Multiply by 100 and reduce the fraction.
    c. Divide the numerator by the denominator.
    d. Divide by 100 and reduce the fraction.

18. Which expression is the result of simplifying the following equation?
$(4x^2 + 3x - 7) + (2x^2 - x + 5)$
    a. $6x^2 + 3x - 2$
    b. $6x^2 + 2x - 2$
    c. $4x^2 + 2x - 2$
    d. $6x^2 + 2x + 2$

19. Emma works at a department store. She makes $50 per shift plus a commission of $5 on each sale (s) she makes during that shift. Which equation could be used to find out the total (t) Emma makes per shift?

    a. $t = 5 + 50s$

    b. $t = 5 + 50 + s$

    c. $t = 50 + 5$

    d. $t = 50 + 5s$

20. When evaluating word problems, which of the following phrases represent the division symbol?

    a. More than

    b. Product of

    c. Quotient of

    d. Results in

21. Which of the following choices results from solving the linear equation below?
$2(x - 9) = 2(3 - 2x)$

    a. $x = 4$

    b. $x = 3.75$

    c. $x = 3$

    d. $x = 8$

22. What would be the next term in the following sequence?
$3, 9, 27, 81 \ldots$

    a. 243

    b. 90

    c. 135

    d. 323

23. Which two measurements of a triangle are needed to calculate the area of the triangle?

    a. Length, width

    b. Base, height

    c. Perimeter, height

    d. Base, width

24. Which of the following is a true statement regarding a line?

    a. A line has thickness.

    b. A line ends at two points.

    c. A line connects two points.

    d. A line and a line segment are the same thing.

25. What is an angle measuring less than 90 degrees called?

    a. Obtuse

    b. Right

    c. Complementary

    d. Acute

26. Which of the following units would be most appropriate to measure the size of a book?
    a. Millimeters
    b. Feet
    c. Yards
    d. Inches

27. Which of the following lists U.S. customary units for volume of liquids from largest to smallest?
    a. Fluid ounces, cup, pint, quart, gallon
    b. Gallon, quart, pint, cup, fluid ounces
    c. Gallon, quart, pint, fluid ounces, cup
    d. Quart, gallon, pint, cup, fluid ounces

28. Morgan wants to exercise at least 3 hours total this week. He exercised 35 minutes on Monday, 22 minutes on Tuesday, 41 minutes on Wednesday, and 1 hour on Thursday. How many more minutes does Morgan need to exercise to reach his goal of 3 hours?
    a. 22
    b. 81
    c. 25
    d. 44

29. Which of the following measure of central tendency is the data point in the middle of the sample when arranged in numerical order?
    a. Mean
    b. Mode
    c. Median
    d. Range

30. What is the mode of the following data set?
22, 18, 46, 37, 46, 25, 18, 33, 46, 25, 41
    a. 18
    b. 25
    c. 46
    d. 33

31. What is a data point with a value either extremely large or extremely small compared to the other values in a set?
    a. Gap
    b. Outlier
    c. Kurtosis
    d. Spread

32. In the following scatter plot, what type of correlation is present?

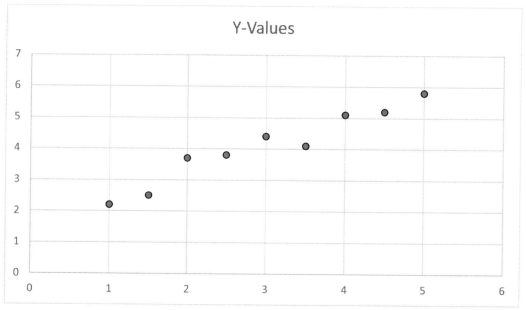

a. Positive
b. Negative
c. Independent
d. No correlation is present

33. In the following bar graph, how many children prefer brownies and cake?

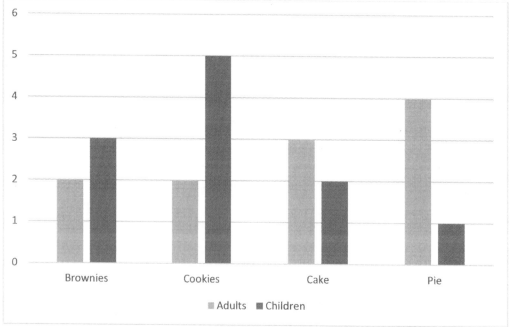

a. 3
b. 4
c. 7
d. 5

34. Which of the following graphs represents each category as a percentage of the whole data set?
    a. Line graph
    b. Circle graph
    c. Bar graph
    d. Box plot

35. Riley has 4 red shirts, 5 pink shirts, 2 blue shirts, 4 white shirts, and 1 black shirt. She pulls one out of her closet without looking. What is the probability she will pull out a white shirt?
    a. $\frac{1}{16}$
    b. $\frac{1}{4}$
    c. $\frac{1}{8}$
    d. $\frac{3}{16}$

36. What type of event is represented by a scenario where the first event does not affect the result of the second event?
    a. Likely
    b. Dependent
    c. Independent
    d. Unlikely

37. Which of the following is a three-dimensional shape?
    a. Circle
    b. Triangle
    c. Hexagon
    d. Cube

38. Trevor went to buy school supplies. He spent a total of $18.25. He bought 3 notebooks, 2 packages of paper, and 1 pencil sharpener. How many boxes of pens did he buy?

Item	Cost
Notebook	$2.75
Package of paper	$1.50
Pencil sharpener	$3.00
Box of pens	$2.00

    a. 2
    b. 3
    c. 4
    d. 5

Quantitative Reasoning Answer Explanations

1. A: Using the order of operations, multiplication and division are computed first from left to right. Multiplication is on the left; therefore, the teacher should perform multiplication first.

2. B: A number is prime because its only factors are itself and one. Positive numbers (greater than zero) can be prime numbers.

3. A: Order of operations follows PEMDAS—Parentheses, Exponents, Multiplication and Division from left to right, and Addition and Subtraction from left to right.

4. A: The place value to the right of the thousandth place, which would be the ten-thousandth place, is what gets utilized. The value in the thousandth place is 7. The number in the place value to its right is greater than 4, so the 7 gets bumped up to 8. Everything to its right turns to a zero, to get 245.2680. The zero is dropped because it is part of the decimal.

5. B: This is a division problem because the original amount needs to be split up into equal amounts. The mixed number $12\frac{1}{2}$ should be converted to an improper fraction first. $12\frac{1}{2} = (12 \times 2) + \frac{1}{2} = \frac{23}{2}$. Carey needs determine how many times $\frac{23}{2}$ goes into 184. This is a division problem: $184 \div \frac{23}{2} = ?$ The fraction can be flipped, and the problem turns into the multiplication: $184 \times \frac{2}{23} = \frac{368}{23}$. This improper fraction can be simplified into 16 because $368 \div 23 = 16$. The answer is 16 lawn segments.

6. C: Numbers should be lined up by decimal places before subtraction is performed. This is because subtraction is performed within each place value. The other operations, such as multiplication, division, and exponents (which is a form of multiplication), involve ignoring the decimal places at first and then including them at the end.

7. A: The additive and subtractive identity is zero. When added or subtracted to any number, zero does not change the original number.

8. B: A rectangle is a specific type of parallelogram. It has 4 right angles. A square is a rhombus that has 4 right angles. Therefore, a square is always a rectangle because it has two sets of parallel lines and 4 right angles.

9. C: Volume of this 3-dimensional figure is calculated using length x width x height. Each measure of length is in inches. Therefore, the answer would be labeled in cubic inches.

10. A: A common denominator must be found. The least common denominator is 15 because it has both 5 and 3 as factors. The fractions must be rewritten using 15 as the denominator.

11. B: Perimeter of a rectangle is the sum of all four sides. Therefore, the answer is $P = 14 + 8\,{}^{1}/_{2} + 14 + 8\,{}^{1}/_{2} = 14 + 14 + 8 + {}^{1}/_{2} + 8 + {}^{1}/_{2} = 45$ square inches.

12. C: Inches, pounds, and baking measurements, such as tablespoons, are not part of the metric system. Kilograms, grams, kilometers, and meters are part of the metric system.

13. C: It shows the associative property of multiplication. The order of multiplication does not matter, and the grouping symbols do not change the final result once the expression is evaluated.

14. C: A compass is a tool that can be used to draw a circle. The compass would be drawn by using the length of the radius, which is half of the diameter.

15. B: Ordinal numbers represent a ranking. Placing second in a competition is a ranking among the other participants of the spelling bee.

16. A: The expanded or decomposed form represents the sum of each place value of a number. The numbers are added back together to find the standard form of the number.

17. C: The method used to convert a fraction to a decimal is to divide the numerator by the denominator.

18. B: When adding algebraic expressions, the parentheses can be removed. Next, like terms are combined by adding the coefficients of each variable together.

19. D: Algebraic expressions can be used with unknown quantities to create equations that represent real-world situations. In this example, the $50 per shift amount would be added to the commission amount of $5 times the amount of sales per shift to reach the total.

20. C: Phrases such as divided by, quotient of, or half of can all be used to indicate the use of the division symbol in a mathematical expression. More than typically indicates the addition symbol. The multiplication symbol is represented by the phrase product of. Results in is another way to say equal to and is shown by the equal sign.

21. A: The linear equation can be solved by first using the distributive property which results in $2x - 18 = 6 - 4x$. The next step is to combine the like terms resulting in $6x = 24$. The final step is to divide both sides by 6 to find $x = 4$.

22. A: The sequence presented is a geometric sequence where each step is multiplied by 3 to get the next subsequent step. $81 \times 3 = 243$, so the correct answer is 243.

23. B: The correct formula for calculating the area of a triangle is $A = \frac{1}{2} \times b \times h$, where A is equal to area, b is equal to base, and h is equal to height. Therefore, the two measurements needed to calculate the area of a triangle are base and height.

24. C: A line does connect two points, but it extends indefinitely in both directions. If the line does end at the two points, then it is a line segment. A line also has no thickness.

25. D: An angle measuring less than 90 degrees is called an acute angle. An angle measuring more than 90 degrees is an obtuse angle. A right angle is an angle that measures 90 degrees. A complementary angle is one of two angles which when added together equal 90 degrees.

26. D: The most appropriate unit to use when measuring the size of a book is inches. This is based on the knowledge of the approximate size of most books and knowing the approximate size of the unit of measurement. Both yards and feet are too large, while millimeters are too small.

27. B: The U.S. customary units of measurement for volume of liquids is from largest to smallest: gallon, quart, pint, cup, and fluid ounces.

28. A: Morgan will need to do 22 more minutes of exercise to reach his goal of 3 hours for the week. The following equation can be used to find the solution. $\left(3 \ hours \ \times \frac{60 \ minutes}{1 \ hour}\right) - 35 \ minutes -$ $22 \ minutes - 41 \ minutes - \left(1 \ hour \ \times \frac{60 \ minutes}{1 \ hour}\right) = 22 \ minutes$. The information given in hours must be converted to minutes so the amounts can be used to solve the equation.

29. C: The median in a data set is the data point found in the middle of the set when arranged in numerical order from least to greatest. The mean is the average of a data set. The mode is the value that occurs the most in a data set. Range refers to the spread of values in a data set.

30. C: The mode of a data set is 46 because it appears most often. In this data set, there are three 46's which is more than any other value. 18 and 25 both appear only twice in the sample. 33 is the median of the data set.

31. B: A data point that is very large or very small comparatively to the other values in the data set is an outlier. A gap is an interval in the range of a data set where there are no data points. Kurtosis measures whether data has a high or low number of outliers. Spread represents how far data points are from the center of a set.

32. A: The correlation between the two variables in this scatter plot is positive because the line of best-fit that can be drawn would have a positive slope. If the correlation was negative, the line of best-fit would have a negative slope. Independent refers to the variables on the x-axis and does not address correlation. If the data points were not in a linear formation, and no line of best-fit could be drawn, there would be no correlation.

33. D: In this bar graph, 5 children prefer brownies and cake. The children columns for brownies and cake have heights of 3 and 2, respectively. Added together that makes a total of 5 children.

34. B: A circle graph does not show the frequency of the individual categories, but rather indicates how much of the whole set (the percentage) is represented by each category. A line graph and a bar graph both demonstrate the frequency of each category within a data set. A box plot divides a data set into quartiles.

35. B: There are 16 shirts in all and 4 white shirts, so the probability of randomly choosing a white shirt is $\frac{4}{16} = \frac{1}{4}$.

36. C: Independent events are situations where the outcome of the first event has no impact on the outcome of the second event. Likely and unlikely refer to the chance an event will occur or not. Dependent events have outcomes that do affect one another.

37. D: A cube is a three-dimensional solid shape. Two-dimensional shapes are flat like circles, triangles, hexagons, squares, and other similar shapes.

38. A: Trevor bought 2 boxes of pens. If he bought 3 notebooks, 2 packages of paper, and 1 pencil sharpener, then he spent $8.25, $3, and $3 on those items respectively. The total of those items then is $14.25. The difference between the total of those items and the total spent of $18.25 is $4. Therefore, he bought 2 boxes of pens at $2 apiece for $4.

Math Achievement Practice Questions

1. Which of the following is equivalent to the value of the digit 3 in the number 792.134?
   a. 3×10
   b. 3×100
   c. $\frac{3}{10}$
   d. $\frac{3}{100}$

2. How will the following number be written in standard form: $(1 \times 10^4) + (3 \times 10^3) + (7 \times 10^1) + (8 \times 10^0)$
   a. 137
   b. 13,078
   c. 1,378
   d. 8,731

3. How will the number 847.89632 be written if rounded to the nearest hundredth?
   a. 847.90
   b. 900
   c. 847.89
   d. 847.896

4. What is the value of the sum of $\frac{1}{3}$ and $\frac{2}{5}$?
   a. $\frac{3}{8}$
   b. $\frac{11}{15}$
   c. $\frac{11}{30}$
   d. $\frac{4}{5}$

5. What is the value of the expression: $7^2 - 3 \times (4 + 2) + 15 \div 5$?
   a. 12.2
   b. 40.2
   c. 34
   d. 58.2

6. How will $\frac{4}{5}$ be written as a percent?
   a. 40%
   b. 125%
   c. 90%
   d. 80%

7. If Danny takes 48 minutes to walk 3 miles, how long should it take him to walk 5 miles maintaining the same speed?

   a. 32 min

   b. 64 min

   c. 80 min

   d. 96 min

8. What are all the factors of 12?

   a. 12, 24, 36

   b. 1, 2, 4, 6, 12

   c. 12, 24, 36, 48

   d. 1, 2, 3, 4, 6, 12

9. A construction company is building a new housing development with the property of each house measuring 30 feet wide. If the length of the street is zoned off at 345 feet, how many houses can be built on the street?

   a. 11

   b. 115

   c. 11.5

   d. 12

10. How will the following algebraic expression be simplified: $(5x^2 - 3x + 4) - (2x^2 - 7)$?

   a. x^5

   b. $3x^2 - 3x + 11$

   c. $3x^2 - 3x - 3$

   d. $x - 3$

11. Kassidy drove for 3 hours at a speed of 60 miles per hour. Using the distance formula, $d = r \times t$ ($distance = rate \times time$), how far did Kassidy travel?

   a. 20 miles

   b. 180 miles

   c. 65 miles

   d. 120 miles

12. If $-3(x + 4) \geq x + 8$, what is the value of x?

   a. $x = 4$

   b. $x \geq 2$

   c. $x \geq -5$

   d. $x \leq -5$

13. Karen gets paid a weekly salary and a commission for every sale that she makes. The table below shows the number of sales and her pay for different weeks.

Sales	2	7	4	8
Pay	$380	$580	$460	$620

Which of the following equations represents Karen's weekly pay?
    a. $y = 90x + 200$
    b. $y = 90x - 200$
    c. $y = 40x + 300$
    d. $y = 40x - 300$

14. Which inequality represents the values displayed on the number line?

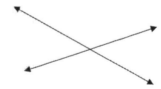

    a. $x < 1$
    b. $x \leq 1$
    c. $x > 1$
    d. $x \geq 1$

15. What is the 42nd item in the pattern: ▲○○□▲○○□▲…?
    a. ○
    b. ▲
    c. □
    d. None of the above

16. Which of the following statements is true about the two lines below?

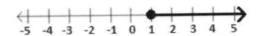

    a. The two lines are parallel but not perpendicular.
    b. The two lines are perpendicular but not parallel.
    c. The two lines are both parallel and perpendicular.
    d. The two lines are neither parallel nor perpendicular.

17. Which of the following figures is not a polygon?
    a. Decagon
    b. Cone
    c. Triangle
    d. Rhombus

18. What is the area of the regular hexagon shown below?

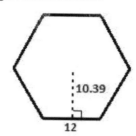

10.39

12

    a. 72
    b. 124.68
    c. 374.04
    d. 748.08

19. The area of a given rectangle is 24 centimeters. If the measure of each side is multiplied by 3, what is the area of the new figure?
    a. 48cm
    b. 72cm
    c. 216cm
    d. 13,824cm

20. What are the coordinates of the point plotted on the grid?

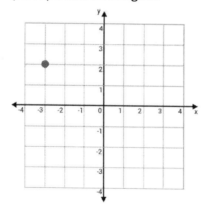

    a. (-3, 2)
    b. (2, -3)
    c. (-3, -2)
    d. (2, 3)

21. The perimeter of a 6-sided polygon is 56 cm. The length of three sides is 9 cm each. The length of two other sides is 8 cm each. What is the length of the missing side?
    a. 11 cm
    b. 12 cm
    c. 13 cm
    d. 10 cm

22. Katie works at a clothing company and sold 192 shirts over the weekend. $1/3$ of the shirts that were sold were patterned, and the rest were solid. Which mathematical expression would calculate the number of solid shirts Katie sold over the weekend?

    a. $192 \times \frac{1}{3}$

    b. $192 \div \frac{1}{3}$

    c. $192 \times (1 - \frac{1}{3})$

    d. $192 \div 3$

23. Which measure for the center of a small sample set is most affected by outliers?
    a. Mean
    b. Median
    c. Mode
    d. None of the above

24. Given the value of a given stock at monthly intervals, which graph should be used to best represent the trend of the stock?
    a. Box plot
    b. Line plot
    c. Line graph
    d. Circle graph

25. What is the probability of randomly picking the winner and runner-up from a race of 4 horses and distinguishing which is the winner?

    a. $\frac{1}{4}$

    b. $\frac{1}{2}$

    c. $\frac{1}{16}$

    d. $\frac{1}{12}$

26. Last year, the New York City area received approximately $27\frac{3}{4}$ inches of snow. The Denver area received approximately 3 times as much snow as New York City. How much snow fell in Denver?
    a. 60 inches

    b. $27\frac{1}{4}$ inches

    c. $9\frac{1}{4}$ inches

    d. $83\frac{1}{4}$ inches

27. Evaluate $9 \times 9 \div 9 + 9 - 9 \div 9$.
    a. 0
    b. 17
    c. 81
    d. 9

Math Achievement Answer Explanations

1. D: $\frac{3}{100}$. Each digit to the left of the decimal point represents a higher multiple of 10 and each digit to the right of the decimal point represents a quotient of a higher multiple of 10 for the divisor. The first digit to the right of the decimal point is equal to the value $\div$ 10. The second digit to the right of the decimal point is equal to the value $\div (10 \times 10)$, or the value $\div 100$.

2. B: 13,078. The power of 10 by which a digit is multiplied corresponds with the number of zeros following the digit when expressing its value in standard form. Therefore, $(1 \times 10^4) + (3 \times 10^3) + (7 \times 10^1) + (8 \times 10^0) = 10,000 + 3,000 + 70 + 8 = 13,078$.

3. A: 847.90. The hundredth place value is located two digits to the right of the decimal point (the digit 9). The digit to the right of the place value is examined to decide whether to round up or keep the digit. In this case, the digit 6 is 5 or greater so the hundredth place is rounded up. When rounding up, if the digit to be increased is a 9, the digit to its left is increased by one and the digit in the desired place value is made a zero. Therefore, the number is rounded to 847.90.

4. B: $\frac{11}{15}$. Fractions must have like denominators to be added. The least common multiple of the denominators 3 and 5 is found. The LCM is 15, so both fractions should be changed to equivalent fractions with a denominator of 15. To determine the numerator of the new fraction, the old numerator is multiplied by the same number by which the old denominator is multiplied to obtain the new denominator. For the fraction $\frac{1}{3}$, 3 multiplied by 5 will produce 15. Therefore, the numerator is multiplied by 5 to produce the new numerator $\left(\frac{1 \times 5}{3 \times 5} = \frac{5}{15}\right)$. For the fraction $\frac{2}{5}$, multiplying both the numerator and denominator by 3 produces $\frac{6}{15}$. When fractions have like denominators, they are added by adding the numerators and keeping the denominator the same: $\frac{5}{15} + \frac{6}{15} = \frac{11}{15}$.

5. C: 34. When performing calculations consisting of more than one operation, the order of operations should be followed: *Parenthesis, Exponents, Multiplication/Division, Addition/Subtraction*. Parenthesis: $7^2 - 3 \times (4 + 2) + 15 \div 5 = 7^2 - 3 \times (6) + 15 \div 5$. Exponents: $7^2 - 3 \times 6 + 15 \div 5 = 49 - 3 \times 6 + 15 \div 5$. Multiplication/Division (from left to right): $49 - 3 \times 6 + 15 \div 5 = 49 - 18 + 3$. Addition/Subtraction (from left to right): $49 - 18 + 3 = 34$.

6. D: 80%. To convert a fraction to a percent, the fraction is first converted to a decimal. To do so, the numerator is divided by the denominator: $4 \div 5 = 0.8$. To convert a decimal to a percent, the number is multiplied by 100: $0.8 \times 100 = 80\%$.

7. C: 80 min. To solve the problem, a proportion is written consisting of ratios comparing distance and time. One way to set up the proportion is: $\frac{3}{48} = \frac{5}{x} \left(\frac{distance}{time} = \frac{distance}{time}\right)$ where x represents the unknown value of time. To solve a proportion, the ratios are cross-multiplied: $(3)(x) = (5)(48) \rightarrow 3x = 240$. The equation is solved by isolating the variable, or dividing by 3 on both sides, to produce $x = 80$.

8. D: 1, 2, 3, 4, 6, 12. A given number divides evenly by each of its factors to produce an integer (no decimals). The number 5, 7, 8, 9, 10, 11 (and their opposites) do not divide evenly into 12. Therefore, these numbers are not factors.

9. A: 11. To determine the number of houses that can fit on the street, the length of the street is divided by the width of each house: $345 \div 30 = 11.5$. Although the mathematical calculation of 11.5 is correct, this answer is not reasonable. Half of a house cannot be built, so the company will need to either build 11 or 12 houses. Since the width of 12 houses (360 feet) will extend past the length of the street, only 11 houses can be built.

10. B: $3x^2 - 3x + 11$. By distributing the implied one in front of the first set of parentheses and the -1 in front of the second set of parentheses, the parenthesis can be eliminated: $1(5x^2 - 3x + 4) - 1(2x^2 - 7) = 5x^2 - 3x + 4 - 2x^2 + 7$. Next, like terms (same variables with same exponents) are combined by adding the coefficients and keeping the variables and their powers the same: $5x^2 - 3x + 4 - 2x^2 + 7 = 3x^2 - 3x + 11$.

11. B: 180 miles. The rate, 60 miles per hour, and time, 3 hours, are given for the scenario. To determine the distance traveled, the given values for the rate (r) and time (t) are substituted into the distance formula and evaluated: $d = r \times t \to d = (60mi/h) \times (3h) \to d = 180mi$.

12. D: $x \leq -5$. When solving a linear equation or inequality:

Distribution is performed if necessary: $-3(x + 4) \to -3x - 12 \geq x + 8$. This means that any like terms on the same side of the equation/inequality are combined.

The equation/inequality is manipulated to get the variable on one side. In this case, subtracting x from both sides produces $-4x - 12 \geq 8$.

The variable is isolated using inverse operations to undo addition/subtraction. Adding 12 to both sides produces $-4x \geq 20$.

The variable is isolated using inverse operations to undo multiplication/division. Remember if dividing by a negative number, the relationship of the inequality reverses, so the sign is flipped. In this case, dividing by -4 on both sides produces $x \leq -5$.

13. C: $y = 40x + 300$. In this scenario, the variables are the number of sales and Karen's weekly pay. The weekly pay depends on the number of sales. Therefore, weekly pay is the dependent variable (y) and the number of sales is the independent variable (x). Each pair of values from the table can be written as an ordered pair (x, y): (2,380), (7,580), (4,460), (8,620). The ordered pairs can be substituted into the equations to see which creates true statements (both sides equal) for each pair. Even if one ordered pair produces equal values for a given equation, the other three ordered pairs must be checked. The only equation which is true for all four ordered pairs is $y = 40x + 300$:

$$380 = 40(2) + 300 \to 380 = 380$$

$$580 = 40(7) + 300 \to 580 = 580$$

$$460 = 40(4) + 300 \to 460 = 460$$

$$620 = 40(8) + 300 \to 620 = 620$$

14. D: $x \geq 1$. The closed dot on one indicates that the value is included in the set. The arrow pointing right indicates that numbers greater than one (numbers get larger to the right) are included in the set. Therefore, the set includes numbers greater than or equal to one, which can be written as $x \geq 1$.

15. A: ○. The core of the pattern consists of 4 items: ▲○○□. Therefore, the core repeats in multiples of 4, with the pattern starting over on the next step. The closest multiple of 4 to 42 is 40. Step 40 is the end of the core (□), so step 41 will start the core over (▲) and step 42 is ○.

16. D: The two lines are neither parallel nor perpendicular. Parallel lines will never intersect or meet. Therefore, the lines are not parallel. Perpendicular lines intersect to form a right angle (90°). Although the lines intersect, they do not form a right angle, which is usually indicated with a box at the intersection point. Therefore, the lines are not perpendicular.

17. B: Cone. A polygon is a closed two-dimensional figure consisting of three or more sides. A decagon is a polygon with 10 sides. A triangle is a polygon with three sides. A rhombus is a polygon with 4 sides. A cone is a three-dimensional figure and is classified as a solid.

18. C: 374.04. The formula for finding the area of a regular polygon is $A = \frac{1}{2} \times a \times P$ where a is the length of the apothem (from the center to any side at a right angle) and P is the perimeter of the figure. The apothem a is given as 10.39 and the perimeter can be found by multiplying the length of one side by the number of sides (since the polygon is regular): $P = 12 \times 6 \rightarrow P = 72$. To find the area, substitute the values for a and P into the formula $A = \frac{1}{2} \times a \times P \rightarrow A = \frac{1}{2} \times (10.39) \times (72) \rightarrow A = 374.04$.

19. C: 216cm. Because area is a two-dimensional measurement, the dimensions are multiplied by a scale that is squared to determine the scale of the corresponding areas. The dimensions of the rectangle are multiplied by a scale of 3. Therefore, the area is multiplied by a scale of 3^2 (which is equal to 9): $24cm \times 9 = 216cm$.

20. A: (-3, 2). The coordinates of a point are written as an ordered pair (x, y). To determine the x-coordinate, a line is traced directly above or below the point until reaching the x-axis. This step notes the value on the x-axis. In this case, the x-coordinate is -3. To determine the y-coordinate, a line is traced directly to the right or left of the point until reaching the y-axis, which notes the value on the y-axis. In this case, the y-coordinate is 2. Therefore, the ordered pair is written (-3, 2).

21. C: Perimeter is found by calculating the sum of all sides of the polygon. $9 + 9 + 9 + 8 + 8 + s = 56$, where s is the missing side length. Therefore, 43 plus the missing side length is equal to 56. The missing side length is 13 cm.

22. C: $\frac{1}{3}$ of the shirts sold were patterned. Therefore, $1 - \frac{1}{3} = \frac{2}{3}$ of the shirts sold were solid. Anytime "of" a quantity appears in a word problem, multiplication should be used. Therefore, $192 \times \frac{2}{3} = \frac{192 \times 2}{3} = \frac{384}{3} = 128$ solid shirts were sold. The entire expression is $192 \times \left(1 - \frac{1}{3}\right)$.

23. A: Mean. An outlier is a data value that is either far above or far below the majority of values in a sample set. The mean is the average of all the values in the set. In a small sample set, a very high or very low number could drastically change the average of the data points. Outliers will have no more of an effect on the median (the middle value when arranged from lowest to highest) than any other value above or below the median. If the same outlier does not repeat, outliers will have no effect on the mode (value that repeats most often).

24. C: Line graph. The scenario involves data consisting of two variables, month, and stock value. Box plots display data consisting of values for one variable. Therefore, a box plot is not an appropriate choice. Both line plots and circle graphs are used to display frequencies within categorical data. Neither can be used for the given scenario. Line graphs display two numerical variables on a coordinate grid and show trends among the variables.

25. D: $\frac{1}{12}$. The probability of picking the winner of the race is $\frac{1}{4}\left(\frac{number\ of\ favorable\ outcomes}{number\ of\ total\ outcomes}\right)$. Assuming the winner was picked on the first selection, three horses remain from which to choose the runner-up (these are dependent events). Therefore, the probability of picking the runner-up is $\frac{1}{3}$. To determine the probability of multiple events, the probability of each event is multiplied: $\frac{1}{4} \times \frac{1}{3} = \frac{1}{12}$.

26. D: 3 must be multiplied times $27\frac{3}{4}$. In order to easily do this, the mixed number should be converted into an improper fraction. $27\frac{3}{4} = 27 \times 4 + \frac{3}{4} = \frac{111}{4}$. Therefore, Denver had approximately $3 \times \frac{111}{4} = \frac{333}{4}$ inches of snow. The improper fraction can be converted back into a mixed number through division. $\frac{333}{4} = 83\frac{1}{4}$ inches.

27. B: According to order of operations, multiplication and division must be completed first from left to right. Then, addition and subtraction is completed from left to right. Therefore, $9 \times 9 \div 9 + 9 - 9 \div 9 = 81 \div 9 + 9 - 9 \div 9 = 9 + 9 - 9 \div 9 = 9 + 9 - 1 = 18 - 1 = 17$.

Reading Comprehension

Main Idea

It is important to know the difference between the topic and the main idea of the passage. Even though these two are similar, they have some differences. A topic is the subject of the text. It can usually be described in a one- to two-word phrase. On the other hand, the main idea is more detailed. It provides the author's central point of the passage. It can be expressed through a complete sentence. It is often found in the beginning, middle, or end of a paragraph. In most nonfiction books, the first sentence of the passage usually states the main idea. Take a look at the passage below to review the topic versus the main idea.

> Cheetahs are one of the fastest mammals on land, reaching up to seventy miles an hour over short distances. Even though cheetahs can run as fast as seventy miles an hour, they usually only have to run half that speed to catch up with their choice of prey. Cheetahs cannot maintain a fast pace over long periods of time because they will overheat their bodies. After a chase, cheetahs need to rest for approximately thirty minutes prior to eating or returning to any other activity.

In the example above, the topic of the passage is Cheetahs because that is the subject of the text. The main idea of the text is "Cheetahs are one of the fastest mammals on the land but can only maintain a fast pace for shorter distances." While this covers the topic, it is more detailed. It refers to the text in its entirety. The passage provides more details called supporting details. These will be discussed in the next section.

Supporting Details

Supporting details help you understand the main idea. Supporting details answer questions like *who, what, where, when, why,* and *how.* Supporting details can include examples, facts, statistics, small stories, and visual details.

Persuasive and informative texts often use supporting details. In persuasive texts, authors try to make readers agree with their points of view. In persuasive texts, supporting details are often used as "selling points." If authors say something, they should support it with evidence. This helps to persuade readers. Informative texts use supporting details to inform readers. Take another look at the "Cheetahs" example from the page before to find examples of supporting details.

In the Cheetah example above, supporting details include:

- Cheetahs reach up to seventy miles per hour over short distances.
- Cheetahs usually only have to run half that speed to catch up with their prey.
- Cheetahs will overheat their bodies if they exert a high speed over longer distances.
- They need to rest for thirty minutes after a chase.

Look at the diagram below (applying the cheetah example) to help determine the hierarchy of topic, main idea, and supporting details.

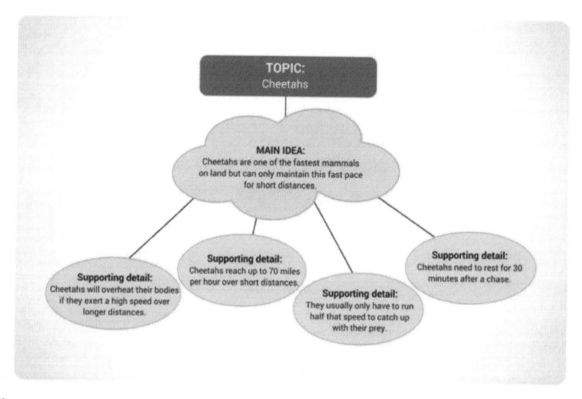

Inferences

When readers put together clues from the writing to "guess" that a certain idea is a fact, it is called making inferences. Making inferences helps read "between the lines" of the writing. Readers read "between the lines" to figure out why the author wrote what they wrote.

Inferences are about being able to make wise guesses based on clues from the writing. People make inferences about the world around them every day. However, they may not be aware of what they are doing. For example, a young boy may infer that it is cold outside if he wakes up and his bedroom is chilly. Or, a girl is driving somewhere and she sees a person on the side of the road with a parked car. The girl might think that person's car broke down, and that they are waiting for help. Both of these are examples of how inferences are used every day.

Making inferences is kind of like being a detective. Sometimes clues can be found in the pictures that are inside of a story. For example, a story might show a picture of a school where all the children are in the parking lot. Looking more closely, readers might spot a fire truck parked at the side of the road and might infer that the school had a fire drill or an actual fire.

Vocabulary/Word Choice

Comparison and Contrast
One writing device authors use is comparison and contrast. Comparison is when authors take objects and show how they are the same. Contrast is when authors take objects and show how they differ. Comparison and contrast essays are mostly written in nonfiction form. There are common words used when authors compare or contrast. The list below will show you some of these words:

Comparison Words:

- Similar to
- Alike
- As well as
- Both

Contrast Words:

- Although
- On the other hand
- Different from
- However
- As opposed to
- More than
- Less than
- On the contrary

Transitional Words and Phrases

There are approximately 200 transitional words and phrases that are commonly used in the English language. Below are lists of common transition words and phrases.

Time	Example	Compare	Contrast	Addition	Logical Relationships	Steps
after	for example	likewise	however	and	if	first
before	in fact	also	yet	also	then	second
during	for instance		but	furthermore	therefore	last
in the middle				moreover	as a result	
					since	

Transitional words and phrases are important writing devices. They connect sentences and paragraphs. Transitional words and phrases help writing to make more sense. They provide clearer meaning to readers.

Interpreting Words and Phrases

Words can have different meaning depending on how they are used in a text. Once a reader knows the correct meaning and how to say a word, they can better understand the context of the word. There are lots of methods for helping readers solve word meanings.

Dictionary: Dictionaries are not allowed on the test. However, readers should know how to use a dictionary and a thesaurus. In dictionaries, there can be more than one meaning for a certain word. Dictionaries also help teach how to say words. A thesaurus teaches words that have the same meanings (synonyms) and words that have opposite meanings (antonyms).

Word Parts: Separating words into their word parts, (root word, prefix, suffix) will help determine the meaning of a word as a whole.

Context Clues: Readers can look at other words in sentences to help them find out the meaning of an unknown word by the way it is used in the same sentence or paragraph. This kind of search provides context clues.

Author's Purpose: Authors use words differently depending on what they want the reader to learn. Some ways writers use words are as follows:

- Literal: the exact meaning of the word
- Figurative: metaphorical language and figures of speech
- Technical: in-depth writing about certain subjects like math or music
- Connotative: showing an opinion in the text as a secondary meaning

Organization/Logic

Organization of Text Structures
Text structures are used for different reasons in writing. Each text structure has key words and elements that help identify it. Readers use text structure to help find information within a text. Summarizing requires knowledge of the text structure of a piece of writing. Here are some common text structures that writers use to organize their text:

Chronological Order: Time order or sequence from one point to another. Dates and times might be used, or bullets and numbering. Possible key words: *first, next, then, after, later, finally, before, preceding, following*

Cause and Effect: Showing how causes lead to effects. Possible key words: *cause, effect, consequently, as a result, due to, in order to, because of, therefore, so, leads to, if/then*

Problem and Solution: Talks about a problem in detail and gives solutions to the problem. Possible key words: *difficulty, problem, solve, solution, possible, therefore, if/then, challenge*

Compare and Contrast: Talks about how objects, people, places, and ideas might be the same or different from each other. Possible key words: *like, unlike, similar to, in contrast, on the other hand, whereas, while, although, either or, opposed to, different from, instead*

Description: Explains a topic with the main idea and details. Possible key words: *for example, such as, for instance, most importantly, another, such as, next to, on top of, besides*

Tone/Style/Figurative Language

Tone
The words authors choose to use must always be well thought out. Although words carry specific meanings, they also carry *connotations*—emotional feelings that are evoked by the words. Connotation creates the tone of the writing. Some words can be said to be loaded words or trigger words that ignite strong emotional responses in readers. These two sentences offer examples:

My grandfather is a robust, elderly man.

My grandfather is a chubby, old man.

In the first sentence, the adjectives used to describe the grandfather instill positive emotions in the reader. However, in the second sentence, the adjectives instill negative emotions. The *mood* of a writing piece refers to the emotions—positive or negative—the reader feels during and after reading. *Tone* refers to the author's purposeful choice of words, designed to evoke those feelings.

Style
Style can include any number of technical writing choices. A few examples of style choices include:

- Sentence Construction: When presenting facts, does the writer use shorter sentences to create a quicker sense of the supporting evidence, or do they use longer sentences to elaborate and explain the information?

- Technical Language: Does the writer use jargon to demonstrate their expertise in the subject, or do they use ordinary language to help the reader understand things in simple terms?

- Formal Language: Does the writer refrain from using contractions such as *won't* or *can't* to create a more formal tone, or do they use a colloquial, conversational style to connect to the reader?

- Formatting: Does the writer use a series of shorter paragraphs to help the reader follow a line of argument, or do they use longer paragraphs to examine an issue in great detail and demonstrate their knowledge of the topic?

Figurative Language
Figurative language is a specific style of speaking or writing that uses tools for a variety of effects. It entertains readers, ignites imagination, and promotes creativity. Instead of writing in realistic terms or

literal terms, figurative language plays with words and prompts readers to infer the underlying meaning. There are seven types of figurative language:

Type	Definition	Example
Personification	Giving animate qualities to an inanimate object	The tree stood tall and still, staring up at the sky.
Simile	The comparison of two unlike things using connecting words	Your eyes are as blue as the ocean.
Metaphor	The comparison of two unlike things without the use of connecting words	She was in the twilight of her years.
Hyperbole	An over-exaggeration	I could eat a million of these cookies!
Alliteration	The patterned repetition of an initial consonant sound	The bunnies are bouncing in baskets.
Onomatopoeia	Words that are formed by using the very sound associated with the word itself	"Drip, drip, drip" went the kitchen faucet.
Idioms	Common sayings that carry a lesson or meaning that must be inferred	That math work was a piece of cake!

Interpretation

Since idioms and hyperboles are commonly used in everyday speech, educators may wish to introduce them early.

I'm so tired that I could sleep forever!—Hyperbole

He's not playing with a full deck!—Idiom

Other forms of figurative language can be found in poetry and in children's stories. As educators come across figurative speech, they can prompt children's critical thinking skills by asking what they think the author meant by those words or that particular sentence. Giving concrete examples of each style and challenging children to attempt writing their very own creative sentences will strengthen their understanding and application of figurative language.

A   O

red green can make pies | Both Fruit & seeds | orange Citrus no pies

Both apples and oranges are fruits & have seeds, while apples can be baked in pies, orange cannot in pies, orange cannot oranges are messy, whereas apples are neat

94

Practice Questions

Questions 1 – 5 are based on the following passage.

Christopher Columbus is often credited for discovering America. This is incorrect. First, it is impossible to "discover" something where people already live; however, Christopher Columbus did explore places in the New World that were previously untouched by Europe, so the term "explorer" would be more accurate. Another correction must be made, as well: Christopher Columbus was not the first European explorer to reach the present day Americas! Rather, it was Leif Erikson who first came to the New World and contacted the natives, nearly five hundred years before Christopher Columbus.

Leif Erikson, the son of Erik the Red (a famous Viking outlaw and explorer in his own right), was born in either 970 or 980, depending on which historian you seek. His own family, though, did not raise Leif, which was a Viking tradition. Instead, one of Erik's prisoners taught Leif reading and writing, languages, sailing, and weaponry. At age 12, Leif was considered a man and returned to his family. He killed a man during a dispute shortly after his return, and the council banished the Erikson clan to Greenland.

In 999, Leif left Greenland and traveled to Norway where he would serve as a guard to King Olaf Tryggvason. It was there that he became a convert to Christianity. Leif later tried to return home with the intention of taking supplies and spreading Christianity to Greenland, however his ship was blown off course and he arrived in a strange new land: present day Newfoundland, Canada.

When he finally returned to his adopted homeland Greenland, Leif consulted with a merchant who had also seen the shores of this previously unknown land we now know as Canada. The son of the legendary Viking explorer then gathered a crew of 35 men and set sail. Leif became the first European to touch foot in the New World as he explored present-day Baffin Island and Labrador, Canada. His crew called the land Vinland since it was plentiful with grapes.

During their time in present-day Newfoundland, Leif's expedition made contact with the natives whom they referred to as Skraelings (which translates to "wretched ones" in Norse). There are several secondhand accounts of their meetings. Some contemporaries described trade between the peoples. Other accounts describe clashes where the Skraelings defeated the Viking explorers with long spears, while still others claim the Vikings dominated the natives. Regardless of the circumstances, it seems that the Vikings made contact of some kind. This happened around 1000, nearly five hundred years before Columbus famously sailed the ocean blue.

Eventually, in 1003, Leif set sail for home and arrived at Greenland with a ship full of timber.

In 1020, seventeen years later, the legendary Viking died. Many believe that Leif Erikson should receive more credit for his contributions in exploring the New World.

1. Which of the following best describes how the author generally presents the information?
   a. Chronological order
   b. Comparison-contrast
   c. Cause-effect
   d. Conclusion-premises

2. Which of the following is an opinion, rather than historical fact, expressed by the author?

    a. Leif Erikson was definitely the son of Erik the Red; however, historians debate the year of his birth.

    b. Leif Erikson's crew called the land Vinland since it was plentiful with grapes.

    c. Leif Erikson deserves more credit for his contributions in exploring the New World.

    d. Leif Erikson explored the Americas nearly five hundred years before Christopher Columbus.

3. Which of the following most accurately describes the author's main conclusion?

    a. Leif Erikson is a legendary Viking explorer.

    b. Leif Erikson deserves more credit for exploring America hundreds of years before Columbus.

    c. Spreading Christianity motivated Leif Erikson's expeditions more than any other factor.

    d. Leif Erikson contacted the natives nearly five hundred years before Columbus.

4. Which of the following best describes the author's intent in the passage?

    a. To entertain

    b. To inform

    c. To alert

    d. To suggest

5. Which of the following can be logically inferred from the passage?

    a. The Vikings disliked exploring the New World.

    b. Leif Erikson's banishment from Iceland led to his exploration of present-day Canada.

    c. Leif Erikson never shared his stories of exploration with the King of Norway.

    d. Historians have difficulty definitively pinpointing events in the Vikings' history.

Questions 6 – 8 are based on the following passage.

Smoking tobacco products is terribly destructive. A single cigarette contains over 4,000 chemicals, including 43 known carcinogens and 400 deadly toxins. Some of the most dangerous ingredients include tar, carbon monoxide, formaldehyde, ammonia, arsenic, and DDT. Smoking can cause numerous types of cancer including throat, mouth, nasal cavity, esophagus, stomach, pancreas, kidney, bladder, and cervical.

Cigarettes contain a drug called nicotine, one of the most addictive substances known to man. Addiction is defined as a compulsion to seek the substance despite negative consequences. According to the National Institute of Drug Abuse, nearly 35 million smokers expressed a desire to quit smoking in 2015; however, more than 85 percent of those addicts will not achieve their goal. Almost all smokers regret picking up that first cigarette. You would be wise to learn from their mistake if you have not yet started smoking.

According to the U.S. Department of Health and Human Services, 16 million people in the United States presently suffer from a smoking-related condition and nearly nine million suffer from a serious smoking-related illness. According to the Centers for Disease Control and Prevention (CDC), tobacco products cause nearly six million deaths per year. This number is projected to rise to over eight million deaths by 2030. Smokers, on average, die ten years earlier than their nonsmoking peers.

In the United States, local, state, and federal governments typically tax tobacco products, which leads to high prices. Nicotine addicts sometimes pay more for a pack of cigarettes than for a few gallons of gas.

Additionally, smokers tend to stink. The smell of smoke is all-consuming and creates a pervasive nastiness. Smokers also risk staining their teeth and fingers with yellow residue from the tar.

Smoking is deadly, expensive, and socially unappealing. Clearly, smoking is not worth the risks.

6. Which of the following statements most accurately summarizes the passage?
    a. Tobacco is less healthy than many alternatives.
    b. Tobacco is deadly, expensive, and socially unappealing, and smokers would be much better off kicking the addiction.
    c. In the United States, local, state, and federal governments typically tax tobacco products, which leads to high prices.
    d. Tobacco products shorten smokers' lives by ten years and kill more than six million people per year.

7. The author would be most likely to agree with which of the following statements?
    a. Smokers should only quit cold turkey and avoid all nicotine cessation devices.
    b. Other substances are more addictive than tobacco.
    c. Smokers should quit for whatever reason that gets them to stop smoking.
    d. People who want to continue smoking should advocate for a reduction in tobacco product taxes.

8. Which of the following represents an opinion statement on the part of the author?
    a. According to the Centers for Disease Control and Prevention (CDC), tobacco products cause nearly six million deaths per year.
    b. Nicotine addicts sometimes pay more for a pack of cigarettes than a few gallons of gas.
    c. They also risk staining their teeth and fingers with yellow residue from the tar.
    d. Additionally, smokers tend to stink. The smell of smoke is all-consuming and creates a pervasive nastiness.

This article discusses the famous poet and playwright William Shakespeare. Read it and answer questions 9 – 12.

People who argue that William Shakespeare is not responsible for the plays attributed to his name are known as anti-Stratfordians (from the name of Shakespeare's birthplace, Stratford-upon-Avon). The most common anti-Stratfordian claim is that William Shakespeare simply was not educated enough or from a high enough social class to have written plays overflowing with references to such a wide range of subjects like history, the classics, religion, and international culture. William Shakespeare was the son of a glove-maker, he only had a basic grade school education, and he never set foot outside of England—so how could he have produced plays of such sophistication and imagination? How could he have written in such detail about historical figures and events, or about different cultures and locations around Europe? According to anti-Stratfordians, the depth of knowledge contained in Shakespeare's plays suggests a well-traveled writer from a wealthy background with a university education, not a countryside writer like Shakespeare. But in fact, there is not much substance to such speculation, and most anti-Stratfordian arguments can be refuted with a little background about Shakespeare's time and upbringing.

First of all, those who doubt Shakespeare's authorship often point to his common birth and brief education as stumbling blocks to his writerly genius. Although it is true that Shakespeare did not come from a noble class, his father was a very *successful* glove-maker and his mother was from a very wealthy land owning family—so while Shakespeare may have had a country upbringing, he was certainly from a well-off family and would have been educated accordingly. Also, even though he did not attend university, grade school education in Shakespeare's time was actually quite rigorous and exposed students to classic drama through writers like Seneca and Ovid. It is not unreasonable to believe that Shakespeare received a very solid foundation in poetry and literature from his early schooling.

Next, anti-Stratfordians tend to question how Shakespeare could write so extensively about countries and cultures he had never visited before (for instance, several of his most famous works like *Romeo and Juliet* and *The Merchant of Venice* were set in Italy, on the opposite side of Europe!). But again, this criticism does not hold up under scrutiny. For one thing, Shakespeare was living in London, a bustling metropolis of international trade, the most populous city in England, and a political and cultural hub of Europe. In the daily crowds of people, Shakespeare would certainly have been able to meet travelers from other countries and hear firsthand accounts of life in their home country. And, in addition to the influx of information from world travelers, this was also the age of the printing press, a jump in technology that made it possible to print and circulate books much more easily than in the past. This also allowed for a freer flow of information across different countries, allowing people to read about life and ideas from throughout Europe. One needn't travel the continent in order to learn and write about its culture.

9. Which sentence contains the author's thesis?
    a. People who argue that William Shakespeare is not responsible for the plays attributed to his name are known as anti-Stratfordians.
    b. But in fact, there is not much substance to such speculation, and most anti-Stratfordian arguments can be refuted with a little background about Shakespeare's time and upbringing.
    c. It is not unreasonable to believe that Shakespeare received a very solid foundation in poetry and literature from his early schooling.
    d. Next, anti-Stratfordians tend to question how Shakespeare could write so extensively about countries and cultures he had never visited before.

10. In the first paragraph, "How could he have written in such detail about historical figures and events, or about different cultures and locations around Europe?" is an example of which of the following?
    a. Hyperbole
    b. Onomatopoeia
    c. Rhetorical question
    d. Appeal to authority

11. How does the author respond to the claim that Shakespeare was not well-educated because he did not attend university?
    a. By insisting upon Shakespeare's natural genius.
    b. By explaining grade school curriculum in Shakespeare's time.
    c. By comparing Shakespeare with other uneducated writers of his time.
    d. By pointing out that Shakespeare's wealthy parents probably paid for private tutors.

12. The word "bustling" in the third paragraph most nearly means which of the following?
    a. Busy
    b. Foreign
    c. Expensive
    d. Undeveloped

Questions 12 – 14 are based on the following passage.

The Myth of Head Heat Loss

It has recently been brought to my attention that most people believe that 75% of your body heat is lost through your head. I had certainly heard this before, and am not going to attempt to say I didn't believe it when I first heard it. It is natural to be gullible to anything said with enough authority. But the "fact" that the majority of your body heat is lost through your head is a lie.

Let me explain. Heat loss is proportional to surface area exposed. An elephant loses a great deal more heat than an anteater, because it has a much greater surface area than an anteater. Each cell has mitochondria that produce energy in the form of heat, and it takes a lot more energy to run an elephant than an anteater.

So, each part of your body loses its proportional amount of heat in accordance with its surface area. The human torso probably loses the most heat, though the legs lose a significant amount as well. Some people have asked, "Why does it feel so much warmer when you cover your head than when you don't?" Well, that's because your head, because it is not clothed, is losing a lot of heat while the clothing on the rest of your body provides insulation. If you went outside with a hat and pants but no shirt, not only would you look silly, but your heat loss would be significantly greater because so much more of you would be exposed. So, if given the choice to cover your chest or your head in the cold, choose the chest. It could save your life.

13. Why does the author compare elephants and anteaters?
    a. To express an opinion.
    b. To give an example that helps clarify the main point.
    c. To show the differences between them.
    d. To persuade why one is better than the other.

14. Which of the following best describes the tone of the passage?
    a. Harsh
    b. Angry
    c. Casual
    d. Indifferent

15. The author appeals to which branch of rhetoric to prove their case?
    a. Factual evidence
    b. Emotion
    c. Ethics and morals
    d. Author qualification

Read the statement or passage and then choose the best answer to the question. Answer the question based on what is stated or implied in the statement or passage.

16. There are two major kinds of cameras on the market right now for amateur photographers. Camera enthusiasts can either purchase a digital single-lens reflex camera (DSLR) camera or a compact system camera (CSC). The main difference between a DSLR and a CSC is that the DSLR has a full-sized sensor, which means it fits in a much larger body. The CSC uses a mirrorless system, which makes for a lighter, smaller camera. While both take quality pictures, the DSLR generally has better picture quality due to the larger sensor. CSCs still take very good quality pictures and are more convenient to carry than a

DSLR. This makes the CSC an ideal choice for the amateur photographer looking to step up from a point-and-shoot camera.

What is the main difference between the DSLR and CSC?
    a. The picture quality is better in the DSLR.
    b. The CSC is less expensive than the DSLR.
    c. The DSLR is a better choice for amateur photographers.
    d. The DSLR's larger sensor makes it a bigger camera than the CSC.

17. When selecting a career path, it's important to explore the various options available. Many students entering college may shy away from a major because they don't know much about it. For example, many students won't opt for a career as an actuary, because they aren't exactly sure what it entails. They would be missing out on a career that is very lucrative and in high demand. Actuaries work in the insurance field and assess risks and premiums. The average salary of an actuary is $100,000 per year. Another career option students may avoid, due to lack of knowledge of the field, is a hospitalist. This is a physician that specializes in the care of patients in a hospital, as opposed to those seen in private practices. The average salary of a hospitalist is upwards of $200,000. It pays to do some digging and find out more about these lesser-known career fields.

What is an actuary?
    a. A doctor who works in a hospital.
    b. The same as a hospitalist.
    c. An insurance agent who works in a hospital.
    d. A person who assesses insurance risks and premiums.

Questions 18-21 are based on the following passage.

Do you want to vacation at a Caribbean island destination? Who wouldn't want a tropical vacation? Visit one of the many Caribbean islands where visitors can swim in crystal blue waters, swim with dolphins, or enjoy family-friendly resorts and activities. Every island offers a unique and dazzling vacation destination. Choose from these islands: Aruba, St. Lucia, Barbados, Anguilla, St. John, and so many more. A Caribbean island destination will be the best and most refreshing vacation ever … no regrets!

18. What is the topic of the passage?
    a. Caribbean island destinations
    b. Tropical vacation
    c. Resorts
    d. Activities

19. What is/are the supporting detail(s) of this passage?
    a. Cruising to the Caribbean
    b. Local events
    c. Family activities
    d. All of the above

Read the following sentence, and answer the question below.

"A Caribbean island destination will be the best and most refreshing vacation ever … no regrets!"

20. What is this sentence an example of?
    a. Fact
    b. Opinion
    c. Device
    d. Fallacy

21. What is the author's purpose of this passage?
    a. Entertain readers
    b. Persuade readers
    c. Inform or teach readers
    d. Share a moral lesson to readers

Questions 22-25 are based on the following passage.

Even though the rain can put a damper on the day, it can be helpful and fun, too. For one, the rain helps plants grow. Without rain, grass, flowers, and trees would be deprived of vital nutrients they need to develop. Not only does the rain help plants grow, but on days where there are brief spurts of sunshine, rainbows can appear. The rain reflects and refracts the light, creating beautiful rainbows in the sky. Finally, puddle jumping is another fun activity that can be done in or after the rain. Therefore, the rain can be helpful and fun.

22. What is the *cause* in this passage?
    a. Plants growing
    b. Rainbows
    c. Puddle jumping
    d. Rain

Read the following sentence, and answer the question below.

"Without rain, grass, flowers, and trees would be deprived of vital nutrients they need to develop."

23. In this sentence, the author is using what literary device regarding the grass, flowers, and trees?
    a. Comparing
    b. Contrasting
    c. Describing
    d. Transitioning

24. In the same sentence from above, what is most likely the meaning of *vital*?
    a. Energetic
    b. Truthful
    c. Necessary
    d. Dangerous

25. What is an *effect* in this passage?
   a. Rain
   b. Brief spurts of sunshine
   c. Rainbows
   d. Weather

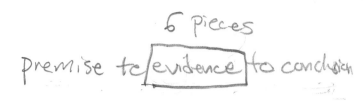

6 pieces

premise to evidence to conclusion

Answer Explanations

1. D: The passage does not proceed in chronological order since it begins by pointing out Leif Erikson's explorations in America so Choice *A* does not work. Although the author compares and contrasts Erikson with Christopher Columbus, this is not the main way the information is presented; therefore, Choice *B* does not work. Neither does Choice *C* because there is no mention of or reference to cause and effect in the passage. However, the passage does offer a conclusion (Leif Erikson deserves more credit) and premises (first European to set foot in the New World and first to contact the natives) to substantiate Erikson's historical importance. Thus, Choice *D* is correct.

2. C: Choice *A* is wrong because it describes facts: Leif Erikson was the son of Erik the Red and historians debate Leif's date of birth. These are not opinions. Choice *B* is wrong; that Erikson called the land Vinland is a verifiable fact as is Choice *D* because he did contact the natives almost 500 years before Columbus. Choice *C* is the correct answer because it is the author's opinion that Erikson deserves more credit. That, in fact, is his conclusion in the piece, but another person could argue that Columbus or another explorer deserves more credit for opening up the New World to exploration. Rather than being an incontrovertible fact, it is a subjective value claim.

3. B: Choice *A* is wrong because the author aims to go beyond describing Erikson as a mere legendary Viking. Choice *C* is wrong because the author does not focus on Erikson's motivations, let alone name the spreading of Christianity as his primary objective. Choice *D* is wrong because it is a premise that Erikson contacted the natives 500 years before Columbus, which is simply a part of supporting the author's conclusion. Choice *B* is correct because, as stated in the previous answer, it accurately identifies the author's statement that Erikson deserves more credit than he has received for being the first European to explore the New World.

4. B: Choice *A* is wrong because the author is not in any way trying to entertain the reader. Choice *D* is wrong because he goes beyond a mere suggestion; "suggest" is too vague. Although the author is certainly trying to alert the readers (make them aware) of Leif Erikson's underappreciated and unheralded accomplishments, the nature of the writing does not indicate the author would be satisfied with the reader merely knowing of Erikson's exploration (Choice *C*). Rather, the author would want the reader to be informed about it, which is more substantial (Choice *B*).

5. D: Choice *A* is wrong because the author never addresses the Vikings' state of mind or emotions. Choice *B* is wrong because the author does not elaborate on Erikson's exile and whether he would have become an explorer if not for his banishment. Choice *C* is wrong because there is not enough information to support this premise. It is unclear whether Erikson informed the King of Norway of his finding. Although it is true that the King did not send a follow-up expedition, he could have simply chosen not to expend the resources after receiving Erikson's news. It is not possible to logically infer whether Erikson told him. Choice *D* is correct because there are two examples—Leif Erikson's date of birth and what happened during the encounter with the natives—of historians having trouble pinning down important dates in Viking history.

6. B: The author is clearly opposed to tobacco. He cites disease and deaths associated with smoking. He points to the monetary expense and aesthetic costs. Choice *A* is incorrect because alternatives to smoking are not even addressed in the passage. Choice *C* is incorrect because it does not summarize the passage but rather is just a premise. Choice *D* is incorrect because, while these statistics are a premise in

103

the argument, they do not represent a summary of the piece. Choice *B* is the correct answer because it states the three critiques offered against tobacco and expresses the author's conclusion.

7. C: We are looking for something the author would agree with, so it will almost certainly be anti-smoking or an argument in favor of quitting smoking. Choice *A* is incorrect because the author does not speak against means of cessation. Choice *B* is incorrect because the author does not reference other substances, but does speak of how addictive nicotine, a drug in tobacco, is. Choice *D* is incorrect because the author certainly would not encourage reducing taxes to encourage a reduction of smoking costs, thereby helping smokers to continue the habit. Choice *C* is correct because the author is definitely attempting to persuade smokers to quit smoking.

8. D: Here, we are looking for an opinion of the author's rather than a fact or statistic. Choice *A* is incorrect because quoting statistics from the Centers of Disease Control and Prevention is stating facts, not opinions. Choice *B* is incorrect because it expresses the fact that cigarettes sometimes cost more than a few gallons of gas. It would be an opinion if the author said that cigarettes were not affordable. Choice *C* is incorrect because yellow stains are a known possible adverse effect of smoking. Choice *D* is correct as an opinion because smell is subjective. Some people might like the smell of smoke, they might not have working olfactory senses, and/or some people might not find the smell of smoke akin to "pervasive nastiness," so this is the expression of an opinion. Thus, Choice *D* is the correct answer.

9. B: But in fact, there is not much substance to such speculation, and most anti-Stratfordian arguments can be refuted with a little background about Shakespeare's time and upbringing. The thesis is a statement that contains the author's topic and main idea. The main purpose of this article is to use historical evidence to provide counterarguments to anti-Stratfordians. Choice *A* is simply a definition; Choice *C* is a supporting detail, not a main idea; and Choice *D* represents an idea of anti-Stratfordians, not the author's opinion.

10. C: Rhetorical question. This requires readers to be familiar with different types of rhetorical devices. A rhetorical question is a question that is asked not to obtain an answer but to encourage readers to more deeply consider an issue.

11. B: By explaining grade school curriculum in Shakespeare's time. This question asks readers to refer to the organizational structure of the article and demonstrate understanding of how the author provides details to support their argument. This particular detail can be found in the second paragraph: "even though he did not attend university, grade school education in Shakespeare's time was actually quite rigorous."

12. A: Busy. This is a vocabulary question that can be answered using context clues. Other sentences in the paragraph describe London as "the most populous city in England" filled with "crowds of people," giving an image of a busy city full of people. Choice *B* is incorrect because London was in Shakespeare's home country, not a foreign one. Choice *C* is not mentioned in the passage. Choice *D* is not a good answer choice because the passage describes how London was a popular and important city, probably not an underdeveloped one.

13. B: Choice *B* is correct because the author is trying to demonstrate the main idea, which is that heat loss is proportional to surface area, and so they compare two animals with different surface areas to clarify the main point. Choice *A* is incorrect because the author uses elephants and anteaters to prove a point, that heat loss is proportional to surface area, not to express an opinion. Choice *C* is incorrect because though the author does use them to show differences, they do so in order to give examples that prove the above points, so Choice *C* is not the best answer. Choice *D* is incorrect because there is no language to indicate favoritism between the two animals.

14. C: Because of the way that the author addresses the reader, and also the colloquial language that the author uses (i.e., "let me explain," "so," "well," "didn't," "you would look silly," etc.), *C* is the best answer because it has a much more casual tone than the usual informative article. *Choice A* may be a tempting choice because the author says the "fact" that most of one's heat is lost through their head is a "lie," and that someone who does not wear a shirt in the cold looks silly, but it only happens twice within all the diction of the passage and it does not give an overall tone of harshness. *B* is incorrect because again, while not necessarily nice, the language does not carry an angry charge. The author is clearly not indifferent to the subject because of the passionate language that they use, so *D* is incorrect.

15. A: The author gives logical examples and reasons in order to prove that most of one's heat is not lost through their head, therefore *A* is correct. *B* is incorrect because there is not much emotionally charged language in this selection, and even the small amount present is greatly outnumbered by the facts and evidence. *C* is incorrect because there is no mention of ethics or morals in this selection. *D* is incorrect because the author never qualifies himself as someone who has the authority to be writing on this topic.

16. D: The passage directly states that the larger sensor is the main difference between the two cameras. Choices *A* and *B* may be true, but these answers do not identify the major difference between the two cameras. Choice *C* states the opposite of what the paragraph suggests is the best option for amateur photographers, so it is incorrect.

17. D: An actuary assesses risks and sets insurance premiums. While an actuary does work in insurance, the passage does not suggest that actuaries have any affiliation with hospitalists or working in a hospital, so all other choices are incorrect.

18. A: Caribbean island destinations. The topic of the passage can be described in a one- or two-word phrase. Choices *B*, *C*, and *D* are all mentioned in the passage. However, they are too vague to be considered the main topic of the passage.

19. C: Family resorts and activities. Remember that supporting details help readers find out the main idea by answering questions like *who, what, where, when, why,* and *how.* In this question, cruises and local events are not talked about in the passage. However, family resorts and activities are talked about.

20. B: Opinion. An opinion is when the author states their own thoughts on a subject. In this sentence, the author says that the reader will not regret the vacation. The author says that it may be the best and most relaxing vacation. But this may not be true for the reader. Therefore, the statement is the author's opinion. Facts would have evidence, like that collected in a science experiment.

21. B: Persuade readers. The author is trying to persuade readers to go to a Caribbean island destination by giving the reader fun facts and a lot of fun options. Not only does the author give a lot of details to support their opinion, the author also implies that the reader would be "wrong" if they didn't want to visit a Caribbean island. This means the author is trying to persuade the reader to visit a Caribbean island.

22. D: Rain. Rain is the cause in this passage because it is why something happened. The effects are plants growing, rainbows, and puddle jumping.

23. A: Comparing. The author is comparing the plants, trees, and flowers. The author is showing how these things react the same to rain. They all get important nutrients from rain. If the author described the differences, then it would be contrasting, Choice B.

24. C: Necessary. *Vital* can mean different things depending on the context or how it is used. But in this sentence, the word *vital* means necessary. The word *vital* means full of life and energy. Choices A and B, *energetic* and *truthful,* do not make sense. Choice D, *dangerous,* is almost an antonym for the word we are looking for since the sentence says the nutrients are needed for growing. Something needed would not be dangerous. The best context clue is that it says the vital nutrients are needed, which tells us they are necessary.

25. C: Rainbows. This passage mentions several effects. Effects are the outcome of a certain cause. Remember that the cause here is rain, so Choice A is incorrect. Since the cause is rain, Choice B—brief spurts of sunshine—doesn't make sense because rain doesn't *cause* brief spurts of sunshine. Choice C makes the most sense because the effects of the rain in the passage are plants growing, rainbows, and puddle jumping. Lastly, Choice D, weather, is not an effect of rain but describes rain in a general sense.

Writing the Essay

Test takers are given thirty minutes to write a short essay in response to a prompt. This section gives test takers the opportunity to show their writing ability as well as show more about themselves. Test takers should be sure to organize their thoughts, prepare a short outline, and write a final copy.

Planning should take place after reading the prompt. This brainstorming stage is when writers consider their purpose and think of ideas that they can use in their writing. Drawing pictures like story webs are great tools to use during the planning stage. Drawing pictures can help connect the writing purpose to supporting details. They can also help begin the process of structuring the writing.

POWER Strategy for Writing

The POWER strategy helps all writers focus and do well during the writing process.

The POWER strategy stands for the following:

- Prewriting or Planning
- Organizing
- Writing a first draft
- Evaluating the writing
- Revising and rewriting

Prewriting and Planning
During the prewriting and planning phase, writers learn to think about their audience and purpose for the writing assignment. Then they gather information they wish to include in the writing. They do this from their background knowledge or new sources.

Organizing
Next, writers decide on the organization of their writing project. There are many types of organizational structures, but the common ones are: story/narrative, informative, opinion, persuasive, compare and contrast, explanatory, and problem/solution formats.

Writing
In this step, the writers write a first draft of their project.

Evaluating
In this stage, writers reread the writing and note the sections that are strong or that need improvement.

Revising and Rewriting
Finally, the writer incorporates any changes they wish to make based on what they've read. Then writers rewrite the piece into a final draft.

Elements of Effective Writing

The following are characteristics that make writing readable and effective:

- Ideas
- Organization
- Voice

- Word choice
- Sentence fluency
- Proper Writing Conventions
- Presentation

<u>Ideas</u>
This refers to the content of the writing. Writers should focus on the topic shown in the picture or prompt. They should narrow down and focus their idea, remembering that they only have fifteen minutes to plan and write! Then they learn to develop the idea and choose the details that best shows the idea to others.

<u>Organization</u>
Many writers are inclined to jump into their writing without a clear direction for where it is going. Organization helps plan out the writing so that it's successful. Your writing should have an introduction, a body, and a conclusion.

Introduction (beginning): Writers should invite the reader into their work with a good introduction. They should restate the prompt in their own words so that readers know what they are going to read about.

Body (middle): The body is where the main thoughts and ideas are put together. Thoughtful transitions between ideas and key points help keep readers interested. Writers should create logical and purposeful sequences of ideas.

Conclusion (end): Writers should include a powerful conclusion to their piece that summarizes the information but leaves the reader with something to think about.

<u>Voice</u>
Voice is how the writer uses words and how they use sentence structure to sound like themselves! It shows that the writing is meaningful and that the author cares about it. It is what makes the writing uniquely the author's own. It is how the reader begins to know the author and what they "sound like."

<u>Word Choice</u>
The right word choice helps the author connect with their audience. If the work is narrative, the words tell a story. If the work is descriptive, the words can almost make you taste, touch, and feel what you are reading! If the work is an opinion, the words give new ideas and invite thought. Writers should choose detailed vocabulary and language that is clear and lively.

<u>Sentence Fluency</u>
When sentences are built to fit together and move with one another to create writing that is easy to read aloud, the author has written with fluency. Sentences and paragraphs start and stop in just the right places so that the writing moves well. Sentences should have a lot of different of structures and lengths.

<u>Proper Writing Conventions</u>
Writers should make their writing clear and understandable through the use of proper grammar, spelling, capitalization, and punctuation.

<u>Presentation</u>
Writers should try to make their work inviting to the reader. Writers show they care about their writing when it is neat and readable.

Tips for the Writing Section

1. Use your time well. Thirty minutes can go by quick! Don't spend too much time doing any one thing. Try to brainstorm briefly and then get writing. Leave a few minutes to read it over and correct any spelling mistakes or confusing parts.

3. Be yourself! You are smart and interesting and teachers want to get to know you and your unique ideas. Don't feel pressured to use big vocabulary words if you aren't positive what they mean. You will be more understandable if you use the right word, not the fanciest word.

Practice Essay Question

Select a topic from the list below and write an essay. You may organize your essay on another sheet of paper.

Topic 1: Who is someone you look up to the most in this world? Why?

Topic 2: If you could move anywhere in the world, where would it be and why?

Topic 3: If you could have dinner with anyone in the world, alive or dead, who would it be? Why have you chosen this person?

Photo Credits

The following photo is licensed under CC BY 2.5 (creativecommons.org/licenses/by/2.5/)

"Black cherry tree histogram" by Mwtoews
(https://commons.wikimedia.org/wiki/Histogram#/media/File:Black_cherry_tree_histogram.svg)

FREE Test Taking Tips DVD Offer

To help us better serve you, we have developed a Test Taking Tips DVD that we would like to give you for FREE. **This DVD covers world-class test taking tips that you can use to be even more successful when you are taking your test.**

All that we ask is that you email us your feedback about your study guide. Please let us know what you thought about it – whether that is good, bad or indifferent.

To get your **FREE Test Taking Tips DVD**, email freedvd@studyguideteam.com with "FREE DVD" in the subject line and the following information in the body of the email:

> a. The title of your study guide.
>
> b. Your product rating on a scale of 1-5, with 5 being the highest rating.
>
> c. Your feedback about the study guide. What did you think of it?
>
> d. Your full name and shipping address to send your free DVD.

If you have any questions or concerns, please don't hesitate to contact us at freedvd@studyguideteam.com.

Thanks again!

Made in the USA
San Bernardino, CA
02 October 2018